Tiger by the Tail

Lord MacLaurin is Chairman of the England and Wales Cricket Board, Deputy Chairman of Vodafone and Deputy Chairman of Whitbread. He has had a long and successful career with Tesco where he was Chairman until 1977. In 1986, at the height of the Guinness affair, he was appointed with four others to the board of Guinness to help unravel the scandal. He was subsequently Chairman of the UK Sports Council.

IAN MacLAURIN

Tiger by the Tail

A Life in Business from
Tesco to Test Cricket

PAN BOOKS

First published 1999 by Macmillan

This edition published 2000 by Pan Books
an imprint of Macmillan Publishers Ltd
25 Eccleston Place, London SW1W 9NF
Basingstoke and Oxford.
Associated companies throughout the world
www.macmillan.co.uk

ISBN 0 330 37371 4

1 3 5 7 9 8 6 4 2

A CIP catalogue record for this book is available from
the British Library.

Typeset by SX Composing DTP, Rayleigh, Essex
Printed and bound in Great Britain by
Mackays of Chatham plc, Chatham, Kent

for Ann

Contents

List of Illustrations

PREFACE

Trading Places

> It's only when you aim for the top that you begin to recognize
> the difficulties involved – whether in business or in sport – of
> formulating a coherent plan, and then motivating others to
> implement it in order to achieve your goal.

I'VE ALWAYS THOUGHT that Alice had it easy in Wonderland.
When asked where a story should begin, she answered with all the
prissiness of a Victorian blue stocking: 'You begin at the beginning and go on until you reach the end.' Which in my case, at
least, resolves nothing, for my life seems to have had so many
beginnings. There was a time when . . . or the instant that . . . or,
as it happened, the occasion on which I first met Jack Cohen in the
bar of the Grand Hotel, Eastbourne, in the summer of 1959.

It was one of those places where discretion's as deep as the pile
of the carpet, and the Old Malvernian touring XI were minding
their own business over a drink before dinner, when this stranger
in evening dress drifted up and handed round his card, saying: 'If
any of you chaps ever want a job, just give me a call.' The brash-
ness was typical of the man. For half a century since he had first
pushed his barrow out of London's East End, 'Slasher Jack' had
been piling it high and selling it cheap, and his chutzpah had
become legendary.

Not that I was unduly interested in his offer, simply curious as

1

to what made this entrepreneur extraordinaire tick. Unlike today, jobs in the late 1950s were easy to come by, though for me there wasn't much job satisfaction to be gained from being a trainee salesman with Vactric, a manufacturer of domestic appliances. It was a job, of sorts, but travelling around in a clapped-out van which had only one proper seat, and with my wife-to-be, Ann, riding in the back in a deckchair didn't hold out too many prospects for the future.

When I got home, a couple of days later, I took up Jack's offer, and gave him a call – to the alarm of my future father-in-law, Edgar Collar, then the Deputy Chairman of Tesco. When I told him what I was about, he was quite adamant: 'I don't want you even to think about joining the company. I've had so much of the Cohen family, I don't want any of my prospective family coming into the business.'

At twenty-three, most of us can be pretty stubborn, and I suspect that Edgar's warning only nerved me in my determination to see for myself just what the no-go area that was Tesco was really about. Which is how I ended up in Jack Cohen's office, being interviewed for a job I didn't really want. It was a bizarre, even surreal experience. There was I, the ex-public schoolboy, and there was Jack behind his huge desk, puffing on the giant cigar that had become his trade mark, and there was this misunderstanding between us:

'D'you want a job?'

'No.'

'Then what are you doing here?'

When I said that I'd taken up his offer merely to satisfy my own curiosity, he came back at me as quick as the hustler that he had always been:

'What are you earning?'

'£900 a year.'

'If you join here, I'll pay you £900, and I'll review the position after six months, and if I like you, and you like me, I'll give you a thousand a year *and* a company car.'

A proper car and a thousand pounds a year! In 1959, it was the limit of my ambition, though when I told my mother that I had accepted Jack's offer she couldn't disguise her horror: 'I haven't spent all this money on your education for you to join a company like that.' The charge was loaded with contempt, but her reaction was typical of the times. As late as the 1950s there was still a deep-rooted prejudice among families like mine against anyone entering 'trade' – the word itself carried its own stigma. There were the usual acceptable occupations for a public schoolboy like myself, but as for retailing, tradesmen were still very much at the back-door of life. I've always felt that the damage that such snobbery has inflicted, not only on our social attitudes but also on our economic performance, has been incalculable – but then, my mother had never been tempted by a thousand pounds a year and a car!

Which, I suppose, is where it all began, the mixed metaphor that has been my life – the one-time cricketer who went into business and who is now back with cricket again. In fact, if cricket has long been employed as a metaphor in business, then business is now being employed as a metaphor in sport.

Since that evening at the Grand in Eastbourne, I've had my share of both, though during those first days at Tesco I never imagined where my own brand of chutzpah would lead. And, God knows, I had little enough time to fantasize, working first as a Warehouse Boy at the company's Epsom store, and then as Assistant Boy – a promotion – to the Store Manager at Tolworth. Then it seemed that this was how it had always been: we rolled up the shutters at nine in the morning, then rolled them down again at five, and if a customer asked for a pound of butter we'd say: 'Hold on a sec, it's in the refrigerator,' then get it from the loo out the back. Now, all this seems to be a world away, which is a measure of the extraordinary changes that have taken place in retailing over the past forty years.

In fact, it is all too easy to forget the accelerating rate of change with which companies are now expected to live, and the demands that this places on them. This applies as much in sport as in business, for the two are virtually synonymous. Once, not so long ago, when Test cricket was still 'just a game' and the 'three box man' (after the weight that an employee could hump around) remained Jack Cohen's yardstick of excellence, it was possible to jog along at a steady old pace, doing very much the same as we had always done. But this is no longer the case, and it was this that was the essence of the Tesco problem. Back in those good-old-bad-old days, Jack Cohen still dominated the company, and he was quite incapable of accepting that the world was changing around him. Indeed, he was so jealous of his power, that he came close to destroying the company he had created.

I was very much an innocent in those early days with the company, but even so, it was obvious that Jack was being overtaken by the times, and that as time passed, he was becoming ever more reactionary. It was a lesson I learned young, and have always remembered: that there is a life-cycle in senior management, and that to hang on to power for too long may be all very fine as far as one's own ego is concerned, but can be enormously damaging to the organization involved. So much is easily said in retrospect, but as I climbed the promotional ladder in Tesco it became increasingly clear that things were far from well in the company. It was not so much Edgar Collar's increasingly despairing remark: 'Never talk to me about the business at home, Ian, I get enough of its aggro at work', more the evidence of the intensifying in-fighting going on at the Board level.

To put it mildly, the atmosphere at the top was poisonous, and the more Edgar, and then Jack's son-in-law, Hyman Kreitman, tried to rationalize the irrational, the more Jack himself resisted. Personally, I've always believed that the sheer effort of trying to educate Jack eventually cost Edgar his life. As for Hyman, he was to become the victim of what only can be described as a vendetta by his own father-in-law. A far-seeing businessman, and undoubtedly the best brain on the Board, everything that Hyman tried to do Jack opposed, to the point where his life had become such a nightmare that he said: 'To hell with all this, I quit.' It was a pyrrhic victory for Jack and Tesco, a company caught in a time trap depending, as it did, on a lot of small profit centres with little overall control.

To some extent the situation mirrors the structure of first class cricket today. I recognize the pride that the counties take in their own independence, and the jealousy with which they guard it, but the reality is that if they can't get the structure of the game right, there is very real danger that they will be faced with the same sort of crisis that Tesco had to confront in the mid-1970s when it seemed that the company might well go to the wall. Indeed, it was very much a matter of touch-and-go when I first joined the Board in 1972. The business was going nowhere, and the City wasn't excited by its prospects for its survival in the intensely competitive sector that retailing has always been. If Tesco was to survive, a revolution was needed which would transform the entire culture of the company – a revolution as much in its management style as in its trading operations; as much in the public's attitude to Tesco, as in Tesco's attitude to itself.

This was the essence of Operation Checkout in 1977: to allow the company to make a clean break with its past, and re-position itself in the market place. The tragedy was that, in the process, it meant breaking Jack Cohen. For him, the very idea of discontinuing Green Shield stamps was anathema. The company had been trading in them for almost twenty years, and for Jack they had become the touchstone of the company's success. By the mid-1970s, however, stamps had passed their sell-by date. A new generation of consumers had emerged, but Jack had as little rational idea of what was going on in the High Street as he had about accepting the fact that people had, indeed, never had it so good. As far as he was concerned, what they wanted was stamps and more stamps. He was determined that Tesco should do a deal with Green Shield, or else . . . The threat was explicit, a part of his management stock-in-trade.

It was a policy that had destroyed Edgar Collar, and broken Hyman Kreitman: Cohen's belief in his own infallibility, and his capacity to wheel-and-deal. Ultimately, it was that belief which made 'Slasher Jack' tick. To wheel-and-deal was all he ever thought about, and I'll never forget that day in March 1977, when we finally managed to force through a vote to drop Green Shield. The meeting over, Jack came into my office, grabbed me by the lapels and raged: 'It's all your bloody idea, and you know who'll be the first to go if anything goes wrong!' I did, and it didn't, for there could be no question about the success of Operation Checkout. In the short-term, Tesco's market share rose dramatically, while in the long-term it provided the company with a platform on which to re-build itself.

In practice, however, the crisis should never have been allowed to arise. I don't believe that any company should ever find itself in a position in which only a palace revolution can save it from its own mistakes. It may be a truism, but as far as I am concerned the successful company is in a state of permanent revolution, of constantly adapting to the myriad changes – social, economic, technological – that conditions its own trading performance. And the faster the rate of change, the more critical the need to take the long view of such developments. The alternative, of pretending that the future is not out there, waiting, is delusory – as Tesco had to learn, and much of the English cricket establishment still have to recognize.

Webbed in tradition, the game had become a caricature of itself, a pastoral scene in which the sun is forever setting on some idyllic county ground, while the home side plays out time until stumps are drawn, and a handful of ageing aficionados remember the time when . . . A nostalgic image, it has diminishing relevance to the competitive world of first class cricket. Which is not to say that I don't share in their nostalgia. I do, for there's nothing I like better than browsing through my *Wisdens* and conjuring up the past. But the reality is that if England is to continue competing effectively at the top level, it is essential that we re-think our whole approach to the game.

In my job with the England and Wales Cricket Board, that's what I'd like to do: to persuade people to have an open mind, to try a few new things, and not retreat into their trenches, because what we have at the moment is not in any way good enough. It is all very well for the establishment to say: 'We'll mind our own business, thank you', when the fact is that not one of the eighteen major counties are financially self-sufficient. It is all very well for them to defend a position where there are 400 paid professionals on the counties' books, when the cricket they play is not sufficiently competitive, and in too many cases only breeds mediocrity. It is all very well to talk-up the past, but as Tesco discovered, the future won't be denied.

In Tesco there is now a tight, top-down management structure, whereas each of the cricketing counties has its own agenda. In many ways, they are like the Co-op, one of the great, traditional institutions in retailing, and a dominant player in the sector, but one in which the devolution of power to the individual profit centres has meant that it has been unable to adapt to the competitive market in which it now has to trade. Which, as I say, is where we were fortunate in Tesco.

Even before that final confrontation with Jack Cohen, I had succeeded in assembling the nucleus of the team that was to revitalize the company. They were a mixed bunch of guys, for I've seen too many management teams drawn from a single social or educational background. When Jack was trying to establish a Cohen dynasty, being 'one of the family' meant much more than being a Tesco employee. If the practice was nepotistic, it certainly was not unique. Management in-breeding takes many forms and while, for instance, the Old Boy approach to executive recruitment – of a Board that all wear the same school tie – may have its attractions, such an exclusive approach has no place when it comes to managing the complex problems of the modern company. What is wanted is a diversity of skills drawn from a diversity of backgrounds – and that was the essence of the team that managed the quiet revolution in Tesco.

In the immediate post-Checkout period, however, we had little idea of where our revolution would lead. I remember sitting down with David Malpas, who was later to become my Managing Director, and a couple of other directors and saying: 'All right, so we've got the tiger by the tail, now what are we going to do with it?' We knew that we had succeeded in stopping the rot, and that our turnover was going right through the roof, but the question remained: How could we consolidate on our success, and build on it into the future? There and then we agreed that we would go into the quality food business, and become the Marks & Spencer of the grocery sector. At the time the conceit was breathtaking. Tesco in the quality food business! The reality of the situation mocked the notion, but having once decided that this was our goal, it provided the motivation for all that was to follow: the quarter century in which Tesco was to become the pace-setter of British food retailing.

Indeed, when we met that day in 1977, we could never have imagined that a time would come when the Chairman of Safeway, Sir Alistair Grant, would say: 'I've got a huge admiration for what you've done at Tesco, and I'm going to copy you in everything you do. I don't care who knows it, I think you've got a bloody good management team, and I'm not ashamed to play follow-my-leader.' Imitation may be the sincerest form of flattery, but I don't think that even Alistair recognized what had been involved in earning his compliment, for while Operation Checkout had provided the initial breakthrough, it was merely the prelude for re-structuring the entire company – top-down and bottom-up. In our thoughts, we might have an idea of where we wanted the company to be, but out there, on the High Street, the public still regarded Tesco as a distinctly tacky operation, and as far as the staff were concerned, the senior management were regarded as a bunch of shysters, or worse.

It was Dr Goebbels who said that every time he heard the word 'culture' he reached for his gun. I know how he felt. There's altogether too much of the word about, not least the variety so assiduously peddled by management consultants. I've always had my suspicions about their worth – after all, if you employ management consultants, why have managers at all? But I have to admit that there is some wisdom in their characterization of company cultures. There is the culture of fear, where no one knows whether their next pay packet will be their last, and the culture of bravado, as typified by 'Slasher Jack'. And then there's the kind of feudal culture that I came across when I attended my first Board meeting at the National Westminster Bank in 1986. As I walked into the foyer of 41 Lothbury, London, the culture of the place weighed me down like a ton of feathers. There was the Commissionaire, as aloof as the Old Lady of Threadneedle Street, until he realized who I was, and then it was: 'May I take your coat, sir? And your bag?

Now if you'll just take the lift to the umpteenth floor, sir', which I did to be served with coffee in the Chief Executive's office by a gentleman in a tail coat. The Board meeting finished, we went upstairs for a lunch that was so extravagant – the silver and the crystal, the wines and the food – that it verged on the obscene. The second floor at Tesco House was far removed from this sort of carry-on. Of course, it's all changed now. Today it's all self-service and getting on with the business. But that sort of self-indulgence was commonplace at the time: a statement personifying the differences between the grandees on the top floor, and everyone else who was expected to grovel to them.

Of course, I'd heard people talking about 'culture shock' before. That first day at the Nat West headquarters, I learned what they meant. To me, the whole set-up mocked the notion of good management. Maybe it is because I had started from the bottom-up in Tesco that I came to appreciate the value of the people with whom I worked – of the couple who managed the first store in which I began my retail career; of the butcher at Staines who taught me to break down a side of beef – or maybe it is simply because I happen to like people. Whatever the reason, I've always believed that the humblest person in an organization is the most important. Ultimately, it is their contribution, multiplied a hundred or a thousand fold, that determines the success, or otherwise of a business. It is all very well for a Board to dream up grand designs – to become the Marks & Spencer of the grocery sector, or the doyen of the Test circuit – but it takes more than a good lunch to put them into practice.

All this I've discovered in the forty years since the day I clocked in as Tesco's first Management Trainee. The title was a misnomer, a figment of Jack Cohen's imagination, for there was no such thing as a training programme in the days when the company was still piling it high, and selling it cheap. Looking back now, however, I realize that I've been on one long learning curve ever since. Today, what I've learned may seem obvious. It certainly didn't at the time. It's only when you aim for the top that you begin to recognize the difficulties involved – whether in business or in sport – of formulating a coherent plan, and then motivating others to implement it in order to achieve your goal. And if and when you're fortunate enough to arrive – and luck should never be traded down – there is always the problem of staying there. Which, I suppose, is what this book is about, the upsides and the downsides (and there can be no escaping the downsides, not least, in personal terms) of trying to take the tiger by the tail, and then hanging on to it.

In my local library there are two shelves devoted to good management practice – erudite works that delight in such titles as *Life Cycle Costing* and *Undertaking Business Process Re-engineering*. It is an encouraging sign. At last, Britain is finally coming to terms with the fact that good management is about more than recycling the past, though I have no intention of joining those self-appointed gurus who spin their theories of 'transaction processing' and 'geometric modelling', of TQM (Total Quality Management) and ES (Exponential Smoothing) but only succeed in making a mystery of the subject. The world is already complex enough, without having to make a secret of what, so often, is a matter of commonsense. Not that Alice found much of it in Wonderland, but, having begun at the beginning, I might as well follow her advice and go on until I reach the end.

CHAPTER ONE

Piling it High; Selling it Cheap

> The tins themselves certainly looked irresistible, all blue wrap-
> pers decorated with a plummy sort of thing, though when, in
> due course, we managers received our quotas, we didn't have a
> clue what they were. They looked like plums, but were they?

I'VE HEARD IT said that the world has changed more in the past
hundred years than it has since the beginning of recorded time.
After thirty-eight years with Tesco, I can believe it. Indeed, after
my first few weeks as a trainee I was willing to believe almost anything. The story then doing the rounds was that 'Slasher Jack' had
created the business in six days, and spent the seventh counting
his profits. The myth captured something of the man, the charis-
matic and seemingly indestructible character who made a practice
of handing out tie clips to visitors engraved with the letters
YCDBSOYA, which he declared to be Yiddish but which, in
reality, stood for 'You Can't Do Business Sitting On Your Arse'. It
was just the kind of vulgarity with which my mother feared I
would be infected, but which, for Jack, was the very essence of his
success.

A Jew, whose parents had fled the pogroms of Eastern Europe
to settle in London's East End, Jack Cohen had served as an air-
craftsman during World War I, only to find himself on the dole
queue following his discharge in 1918. It was an experience he was

never to forget, and it was to condition his business philosophy from the first day he pushed a barrow into Well Street market to 'Pile it High and Sell it Cheap'. The tag was to become a part of the Cohen legend, though it was much more than a simple catch-phrase in the long weekend between the wars when price was the measure of all things, not least of what the unemployed could afford to pay for their food. For half a century, the lessons that Jack had learned peddling God-knows-what from his barrow in the markets of the East End coloured his thinking. In fact, it was just this, his determination to break the inflationary impact of Retail Price Maintenance on the consumer, that was to lead him through the courts in a battle with some of Tesco's major suppliers in the early 1960s.

As a twenty-two-year-old, humping boxes in the Cheshunt warehouse, and later as 'the boy' at Tesco's Tolworth and Epsom stores, I knew little, and cared even less about what motivated The Governor. There was too much work to be done. All I did know, was that it was my good fortune that Arthur Thrush, the company's Retail Director, had decided that if I was to be Tesco's first 'trainee', then I would have to learn the business from the bottom up. There were to be no short cuts, no fast track promotions for me. Either I did the job properly or didn't do it at all, and, for all my mother's reservations, I revelled in it. Maybe I should have gone into one of those respectable professions that she would toll off like beads on a rosary, but I suspect that few would have rivalled the excitement that I found in Tesco.

There is no place for anarchy in business, but anarchy was a part of Jack Cohen's stock-in-trade, a culture in which it was each man for himself provided, always, that he came out on top. While people, such as Arthur Thrush and Edgar Collar, the Finance Director, attempted to rationalize the irrational, Jack would have nothing of it. The quintessential entrepreneur, there was nothing he liked better than to wheel-and-deal. For him, it was what life was all about, whether buying a consignment of tinned milk from a ship that had gone aground on the Goodwin Sands, then distributing it to his stores with the covering note: 'Managers are allowed to use Duraglit to remove any rust from the tins', or wheeler-dealing against his own family to retain control of the business. The fact that times were changing made no difference to him. The one-time costermonger who had made a household name of Tesco, he was as suspicious of the benefits to be gained from the introduction of new management systems as he was quick to dismiss the significance of advanced technology, and I can still hear him chuntering to himself: 'Computers, com-schmuters indeed!'

He wasn't alone in his reservations, of course. As I've since learned, it is all too easy for management to be intimidated by the mysteries of information technology, the more so when its practitioners are agents of the mystification process. Indeed, I've always thought it a little ironic that while they make so much of communication, so many high-tech gurus appear to be incapable of communicating intelligibly with lesser mortals. Not that Jack would have listened even if they had. As far as he was concerned, they could just as well have been speaking in tongues, for he had no more time for their mysteries than he had for any other abstractions. After all, wasn't he Sir Save-a-Lot, the housewife's friend, the self-made legend who had established a retail empire without any assistance from intellectuals, such as his son-in-law, Hyman Kreitman? Business, real business, was about entrepreneurial flair, and as mini-entrepreneurs, each with their own profit centres, his store managers were as happy to subscribe to Jack's enterprise culture as I was delighted when, having been promoted manager of Tesco's Muswell Hill store, I succeeded in doing over £10,000 of business during the Christmas week of

1961. For Jack it was a kind of secular miracle, it had never been done before – in part, perhaps, because for many managers 'buncing' was the name of their game.

For me, that word still evokes memories of those once-upon-a-times when I'd roll up the shutters and open up for business for, back then, buncing was a commonplace practice, a powerful incentive to individual enterprise in a company which lacked virtually any centralized control. When Head Office only conducted stock checks once in every eight or ten weeks, and managers were expected to cover any shrinkage that may have occurred during that period – whether as a result of shoplifting, or from having to dump perished goods – it was generally accepted that they could add a halfpenny on any item under a shilling; a penny on anything between one shilling and two, and whatever they could raise at anything above that. Nominally, the system was designed to cover losses, but tight as Jack was with salaries, managers used it for their own ends, making an art form of the formula: 'One for him, and two for me'. After all, if The Governor made a cult of enterprise, then they would practise what he preached, to the extent that one maestro of buncing called his purpose-built villa on the south coast 'Costa Plenty' – not least, as far as Tesco's returns were concerned.

The practice was typical of the primitive nature of the business. Yet Jack loved it. Tesco was his creation, the product of his initiative. In one way, I suppose that it was sad that he couldn't see that times were changing around him, and that unless he changed with them, all that he had created would be put at risk. Yet there could be no escaping the swash-and-buckle which he continued to inject into the business, or the dynamism of his presence when he'd bustle into one of his then tiny stores (the majority of which were concentrated in London and the Home Counties, and few of which covered more than 600 square feet) to hustle his managers and josh his customers: 'Come on, missus, they're a snip at the price'. Forever the barrow boy, there were always deals to be done. That was his way, the only one he knew. And, since the days when he had first peddled Maconochie's Paste and Lyle's Golden Syrup in London's street markets, since the time he had traded with estate agents to open his first open-fronted stores in the burgeoning suburbs of London in the pre-war years, since he had opened his first, somewhat extravagantly titled 'supermarket' in 1949, it was dealing that had powered his business, and he was damned if he was going to change now.

The questions multiplied as to the cost to the company of Jack's idiosyncratic ways: of the caprice of a self-made millionaire who continued to collect product coupons to fund his winter trips to South Africa; of the chutzpah of The Governor who could never resist a deal and who once bought 100,000 cases of something called 'gambos'. The tins themselves certainly looked irresistible, all blue wrappers decorated with a plummy sort of thing, though when, in due course, we managers received our quotas, we didn't have a clue what they were. They looked like plums, but were they? No one knew, though a quick call around the Tesco network resolved the difficulty. No question, they were plums. So, in 200 stores they were stocked in the tinned fruit section, for doubting customers to be assured that they would make lovely fruit pies. By Monday morning we'd learned how wrong we had been. Gambos, it appeared, were a variety of seeded red pepper, which was how Jack's impetuosity came to ruin the delight of so many families' Sunday lunch!

What Jack practised on a small scale, he continued to practise on a larger one, entering the takeover trail to expand the business. In the early 1960s the retail sector was dominated by a couple of big players, leaving thirty or so other, smaller companies to fight for their market share. Much like Jack, who had entered the business in 1919 with £30 capital, many had developed from such cash-strapped beginnings; and much like Jack, a significant number of them were owned by Jews. A close fraternity, as jealous of their religion as they were proud of their business acumen, they affected a kind of inverted snobbery about their origins, as I was to discover for myself. By 1963, I had risen to the rank of Inspector, and one Saturday morning Jack called me up to ask whether I would care to go with him to Lord's.

'Lord's?' I queried.

'Yes, Lord's. You like cricket, don't you? They're playing the final of the Gillette Cup.'

It was an invitation that couldn't be refused, and as Tesco was one of Gillette's major customers, we were shown into a box in the Tavern Stand, where a seat in the front row had been reserved for Jack. I can see him now, walking down those steps, cheeky as the Cockney sparrow that he was, and stopping every now and then to shake the hand of some startled VIP with the greeting: 'I'm Jack Cohen, and I'm a Jew . . . I'm Jack Cohen, and I'm a Jew.' What do you say to that? I can tell you, the silence was deafening.

When lunchtime came along we all moved to a table at the back of the box where Jack, who was seated at the head of the table, proceeded to feel the lapel of the Chairman's jacket ('Nice bit of stuff that. Who's your tailor?') and then to catechize the rest of the company:

'What are those red and yellow ties you're wearing?', and above the muffle of embarrassment came the reply:

'We're members of the MCC Committee, Sir John.'

'Oh,' says Jack, 'and what does that mean?'

'Well, that we're responsible for the cricket here, for running it.'

'Is that so?' chirps Jack. 'Well, I've never really understood you guys because you only use this place for a few months a year. Now if you had me on the Board, I'd have dog racing round the outside, and dance band concerts in the middle, and if that didn't bloody well pay, I'd pull the whole lot down and build a supermarket.'

In the past couple of years, I've sometimes wondered if he wasn't right. Possibly the cricketing establishment could do with a hustler such as Jack Cohen.

That was not for me to say at the time, though I was coming to realize that Jack's penchant for takeovers was creating nearly as many problems as they solved. On paper, the expansion of Tesco, with the acquisition of companies such as Irwins of Liverpool and Adsega, appeared to make good sense, and the City was certainly delighted with the company's results. In reality, the difficulties of absorbing such alien cultures were formidable. It is a lesson that a lot of companies, Tesco among them, have had to learn the hard way; that while expansion via acquisition in pursuit of growth may appear attractive on paper, the job of integrating a foreign body into an existing culture can cause formidable problems unless handled with a great deal of care – a quality for which Jack was never noted. He would have thought it a waste of his time.

All the old devilry, all the old bravado was there when it came to bargaining for his longtime business rivals. This was wheeler-dealing on a grand scale, though even he was quick to accept that it was going to be 'one hell of a job' to merge the two companies when Tesco took over Victor Value in 1968. It was one of his rare moments of truth, and for the next couple of years I was to live with its consequences. In little more than a decade, Tesco had almost quadrupled in size, the Victor Value takeover having added 217 stores to the Tesco chain, and the problem was to make the new conglomerate work. Each party to the deal operated their own management systems, and each had developed their own trading strategies. The need now was to patch them together, and as a recently appointed Regional Managing Director, that meant working fifteen hours a day, six days of the week for eighteen months. I'd leave home at six or seven on Monday morning, and return on Saturday night, and in any one year I'd cover up to 90,000 miles so that at times it seemed as if home was becoming little more than a Sunday stop-over, a place to recuperate before hitting the road again.

It was then that I began to realize that business can pose hellish choices. It's all very well having ambition, but there's always a price to be paid. At the time, it may not seem like it. At the time, it's all too easy to fool oneself that work's what life's all about, and the justifications come easily: 'You want me to get on, don't you? I'm only doing it for you and the kids.' Come Monday morning I'd say my goodbyes to Ann and the children, an absentee husband and parent. Now I sometimes wonder whether the costs were not too high. Then there was too much to be done to have such doubts. I loved the sheer buzz of the business, careless of the fact that the punishing regime that I set for myself was, in its way, as punishing for the family who only saw me on my Sunday parole from work. Not that Ann ever complained, but sometimes I wonder what she was thinking on those Monday mornings when I took off for God-knows-where, to become no better than a voice at the end of the phone for six days of the week, fifty weeks of the year.

But whilst, eventually, we managed to make some sense of the imbroglio that was the Tesco–Victor Value deal, and whilst the City continued to talk-up Tesco's stock, nothing could disguise the internal problems that continued to dog the company. Against bitter opposition from Jack, Hyman had succeeded in pushing through plans to develop what, at the time, was the most advanced retail warehouse in Europe, at Cheshunt in Hertfordshire, and to open up new and larger stores, whilst closing older ones on a piecemeal basis in the hope that The Governor would never find out, for he remained the autocrat that he had always been. For cosmetic purposes the Board met, discussed, and even came to the occasional unanimous decision, but there could be no question about where power ultimately lay. And the harder Jack was pushed, the more he resisted, caught in a time trap that had little relevance to the present, and even less to the future.

Once it had been all very well to 'pile it high and sell it cheap', but as early as 1959, Harold Macmillan, then the Prime Minister, had talked of people never having it so good, and a new generation of shoppers were becoming increasingly sophisticated in their demands. It is one of those chicken and egg questions as to which came first – whether it was the retailers who created the new market, or was it the customers who demanded better quality shopping? One thing, however, was certain: that for all the best efforts of Hyman Kreitman, Edgar Collar, and Arthur Thrush, and for all the apparent success of the company's acquisition programme, Tesco was still modelled in Jack's image – though there could be no denying the success of what might be regarded as his most audacious deal when he signed up with Green Shield in 1963.

As is so often the case in marketing, it was the Americans who first pioneered the use of stamps, and by 1962 almost half of all grocery sales in the States were covered by stamps. No question, it was a gimmick, but no question, either, that it was a powerful one, and on 29 October 1963, the first Tesco store to trade in Green Shield stamps, opened its doors at Small Heath, Birmingham. Five days later, the *Sunday Express* reported:

Tesco, which launched its Green Shield stamp in twenty-two of its supermarkets last week, has had stamp-collecting housewives swarming around its counters. In Leicester yesterday, the giant Tesco store was besieged by thousands of battling housewives. Twelve women fainted. The staff was completely overwhelmed. Finally, store manager John Eastoe cleared the shop and closed all the doors. Mr Eastoe said: 'I have never seen anything like it in my life. It was quite unbelievable, and quite frightening.'

Ironically, in retrospect, David Sainsbury was to dismiss the Tesco initiative when we launched our Clubcard in 1996, in much the same terms as his predecessor had adopted almost a quarter of a century before: 'They're no better than electronic Green Shield stamps'. Ironic, in that eighteen months later, Sainsbury's were breaking their necks to come in with their own Reward Card. Perhaps David didn't agree with what we were doing, but as I've learned, it's never wise to criticize the competition, because you never can tell when they're going to come back and bop you on the nose.

The huge boost to Tesco's turnover initially provided by Green Shield, however, did nothing to ease the intensifying disputes that racked the Board. The mood was not so much acerbic as poisonous, and the poison reached down into the very heart of the company. Possessive of his power, Jack conducted an uncompromising rearguard action against any attempt to diminish it, and in the process whatever relationship he had once had with Hyman Kreitman became increasingly bitter. Except for their family ties, the two men shared nothing in common: the one the instinctive street trader who was becoming increasingly reactionary as time went by; the other a first class businessman who was trying to save Tesco from its past. Which was exactly what Jack didn't want, and he deployed all his devious skills to frustrate Hyman's intentions. In one respect, in fact, he was much like Ernest Saunders, as I was to discover on being appointed to the Board of Guinness in the autumn of 1986. Neither Cohen nor

Saunders was willing to share the management of power, each regarding it as his own, private purlieu. And in each case, the result was at best unfortunate, at worst, punitive.

Fixed as he was in his ways, Jack neither could, nor would, admit that he, rather than the times, should change, and in the late 1960s, McKinseys were called in, in an attempt to resolve the impasse. I have always had my suspicions about management consultants. They are all very well when it comes to working to a deadline, but all too often they entrench themselves in the interstices of a company, and then they become the very devil to remove. I must say, however, that McKinseys didn't dawdle about reaching their conclusions, possibly because even they found it impossible to unravel the shambolic situation that passed for management at Tesco House. Baffled by what they found, McKinseys coined the masterly understatement that the 'Board does not fulfil its functions in the most disciplined manner', to recommend that it should 'Exercise more self-discipline in interpreting its role and conducting its meetings'.

But if Hyman Kreitman was vindicated, Jack was never to forgive him for the management re-shuffle that followed, in which he was elevated to the titular post of Life President of Tesco, and Hyman became the new Chairman of the Board. Not that Jack gave a damn for protocol. The Board could play musical chairs as much as they liked, but he remained The Governor, and continued to make life hell for his son-in-law, as I was to learn at first hand. In 1971, I was appointed to the Board. It really was an extraordinary set-up, like a meeting of the Chicago mafia, with Jack in the role of the Godfather, all the while scheming to curb Hyman's power. Where the discussions ended, the confrontations began. I'm always amused when I hear people talking about the close bonding of Jewish families. Possibly they were exceptions, but there was certainly no love lost between Jack and his sons-in-law,

Hyman and Leslie. They were constantly at odds with each other to the point where, on one famous occasion, Leslie and Jack grabbed the Wilkinson swords that decorated the Boardroom wall and clashed like duellists, Jack raging: 'One more crack like that, and I'll kill him.'

For all his bloody-mindedness, however, it was extraordinary the loyalty that Jack continued to command. He might be malicious, mean spirited, many things, but the chutzpah still remained, as deceptive as it was beguiling. Daisy Hyams joined the Board at the same time as I did. She had been working for Jack even before the company was founded, and in her own way, she, too, had become a legendary figure in the trade, a highly gifted woman who had established a reputation as one of the toughest buyers in a notoriously tough business. Yet, as I discovered on being asked to rationalize the remuneration of the Board, she was earning only £5,000 to my £7,500. The discrepancy mocked reason. There was I, a comparative newcomer, earning half as much again as one of Tesco's most devoted employees, and one of the key players in the company. When I taxed Jack with the anomaly, however, he was dismissive: 'Oh, she's married. She doesn't need the money'.

Times have changed over the past quarter century, but even then, Jack's response reflected how far he was out of touch with the times. It was not simply meanness, more his belief that women should know their place in the order of things, and that their place was subordinate to men. As outmoded as it was absurd, it was an attitude that was later to lead Daisy to reflect that to be successful in any career, women had to be twice as good as men. A historic prejudice, it has taken far too long to erode. But then, Jack was a compound of prejudices, and it was this that finally broke Hyman Kreitman who resigned the Chairmanship in 1974. The loss to Tesco was as damaging as Jack's delight at having ousted a son-in-law who, for almost thirty years, had been attempting to impose some discipline on his cavalier ways.

In Leslie Porter, Jack believed he had found his natural successor. Not for long, however. A wheeler-dealer much like himself, Leslie's Chairmanship was all too soon to be damned by Jack's jealousy, but where Hyman Kreitman would suffer Jack's spite in silence, Leslie would give as good as he got, whether disputing the ownership of a box of underpants, or the possession of a carriage clock presented to Leslie by Unilever.

Five of us – Jack, Daisy, Jim Pennell (Daisy's Number Two), Leslie and I – had travelled down to Lever Brothers headquarters in Kingston in Leslie's Rolls. After sitting through a formal presentation and lunch, Unilever's Chairman, Len Hardy, presented Leslie with a lovely clock. Now, Jack needed a clock like a hole in the head, but it was the principle of the thing that got to him, and when we got back to the car, smoke was coming out of his ears because Leslie had got the clock, and he had got nothing. He didn't say anything immediately, however, just sat beside Leslie chuntering to himself in the front seat. It was too good to last. Something had to give, and suddenly he turned to Leslie and said: 'You're nothing but a thief and a crook,' and bam, gave him a whack on the shoulder. We were doing sixty or so at the time, and Leslie said: 'Leave off, Governor,' as the Rolls veered across the road. But Jack wasn't to be pacified, and bam, he gave Leslie another whack, at which point Leslie said: 'I've had enough of this,' and punched the Old Man back. Mayhem on the A3, and while Jim Pennell and I tried to intervene, Jack opened the passenger door shouting: 'I know when I'm not wanted. I'm getting out.' Thank God, Jim and I were able to restrain him. Leslie pulled on to the hard shoulder and Jack, still muttering to himself, joined us in the back.

The incident was symptomatic of the troubles besetting the

company. Jack may have wanted to establish a dynasty, but he was as incapable of relinquishing the levers of power as he was of developing a rational line of succession. Always the costermonger, he traded in power as he traded in goods – an item to be chaffered and haggled over, but always with an eye on the main chance. Which, once again, was a part of the tragedy that was 'Slasher Jack': that he had come to believe in the legend of his own indispensability. And so the internecine feuding continued, while Tesco's profits tumbled, and the markets began to ask questions about the company's future prospects if, that is, it had any future at all. And in that, they were not alone. Arthur Thrush taught me many things, but it was from Jack that I learned the dangers of fooling oneself that it is possible to go it alone in business.

I suppose I've always been something of a team player – having captained both the cricket and soccer XIs at school – and since being appointed a Regional Managing Director, I had begun to assemble my own management team to ensure that, as far as possible, my own part of the business was effectively run. They were a mixed bunch, and deliberately so: Colin Goodfellow, who had begun his working life as a butcher's boy, Mike Darnell, who had joined us from Key Markets, and David Malpas, a Liverpool University graduate. I'll never forget my first meeting with David in a pub on the outskirts of Leicester. He was driving a banger of incredible vintage with what passed as an apology for brakes, and as he roared into the car park, he aimed it straight at me, swerved within an inch of my life, then parked and doubled-up with laughter. And I was his new boss! If the omens were not propitious, they were never realized, for a quarter of a century later David was to succeed me as Managing Director of Tesco.

At the time, however, the future was on hold as far as we were concerned, for there were altogether more pressing problems to hand: and stamps symbolized much else that was wrong with the company. By the mid-1970s, it was becoming increasingly clear that they were reaching the end of their useful life. When first introduced, people were thrilled because they were able to save up for all those small, domestic things – toasters and steam irons and such like – and stamps seemed to be an easy way of obtaining them. But as incomes rose progressively, stamps progressively lost their value. And the more they were devalued, the more stamps we gave – double stamps, treble stamps, quadruple stamps – but people still didn't want them; they didn't want to be caught up in the ludicrous game of having to collect a barrow load of books to obtain a TV set. They had better things to do with their time and their money.

But for Jack, stamps were far from being those 'sticky little things' that symbolized the company's problems, and for which Tesco was paying £20 million a year. To him, they had become the icon of his authority – and if Tesco was going to re-position itself in the market, then someone had to play the iconoclast.

CHAPTER TWO

Those Sticky Little Things: Stamps

> Tesco was lumbered with the escalating costs of trading in
> Green Shield from pocket-handkerchief-sized stores. And the
> more of the sticky little things we offered, the less attractive they
> appeared to become.

WHY IS IT that so many authors of books on management make a
literary penance out of what should be a fascinating topic? Surely,
communications should be the name of their game, yet all too
often they make a mystery of the subject, an exclusive preserve to
which only initiates are admitted. Not that Jack Cohen would
have joined them, even if he had been invited. A practising scep-
tic, he had no time for consultants, though he could have taught
the aficionados of management a thing or two about their business, not least, the practice of divide-and-rule. At times, in fact, he
was so leery of his own intentions that he wouldn't let his right
hand know what the left was doing, and the result for Tesco was
chaos.

In the late 1960s, the Board, which was still Jack's fiefdom,
decided to split the company into two, free-standing groups –
Tesco North and South. In theory, the move made good sense.
After a period of rapid expansion, there was a need to devolve
power. In practice, it proved disastrous, for, in dividing up the
company, the Board lost control of a significant element of its

operations. If Jack had not been so keen to play all sides against the middle, and an effective management structure had been in place, all might have been well. The trouble was, that was just his game, and there wasn't any structure. In a culture of every man for himself, Ron Bronstein carved out an empire for himself from his base at Winsford, Cheshire, then the HQ of Tesco's northern operation. At first, all we heard were whispers. Soon they had become the loudest whispers of them all: that to disguise rising levels of shrinkage, Tesco North was operating two warehouses, and 'rotating' merchandise between them whenever a stock check took place.

The situation was symptomatic of much else, and it wasn't helped by the fact that Jim Grundy, a close friend of Bronstein's, had been appointed Chief Executive of the company. It was an extraordinary choice. At times it seemed as if he was verging on the paranoid, going so far as to send registered letters to our homes containing trivial instructions – '*The use of in-store phones by executives is strictly forbidden*'; '*As from today's date, executives should NOT drink tea with store managers*' – each with their tear-off slip to be returned to him personally to show that we had, indeed, got the message. It was difficult enough working for Jack, but he would never go to bed on a quarrel. We would have the most ferocious rows during the day, but he'd always come into my office before going home and say: 'Goodnight, Ian. Tomorrow's another day.'

With Grundy it was different. He was spiteful to the point where life at Tesco was becoming intolerable, and as Managing Director for Tesco South I actively began to think about quitting the company. I suppose the crux of good management is to ensure that the people you work with are on your side, which was not the case with either Grundy or Bronstein. If the former was vindictive, the latter was tactless, once going so far as to say on television that all of Tesco's staff were rubbish, otherwise they wouldn't be working for Tesco. The remark was as much the measure of the man, as of his own and Grundy's management style, and I wanted nothing of either.

In fact, I had gone so far as to look at two or three sites in Bedford, with a view to setting up in business on my own account, before expressing my concerns to Arthur Thrush, not that he needed me to tell him that something was seriously wrong. For more than twenty years he had been involved in a damage limitation exercise to save Tesco from the predatory instincts of The Governor, but they were as nothing compared with the hiatus of the Grundy regime. As Arthur's protégé, things were bad enough for me. As my mentor, they must have been hell for him. Always a manic exercise, it seemed as if the company was running out of control, but all he said when I raised the matter was: 'All right, Ian, leave it to me. I'll see what I can do.' A couple of months later, Bronstein was fired, and Grundy was demoted and posted up north.

Rather than resolving the problem, however, it merely transferred it, and Tesco North's performance continued to deteriorate. By the close of the 1960s, Winsford's profits had all but disappeared, in part, because Grundy continued to ignore the significance of what was happening around him. The first out-of-town superstore was opened in the States in the 1930s, but the idea was slow to catch on in the UK. It seems almost inconceivable now, but as late as 1971 a spokesman for the Consumer Council was saying that even the idea of such developments 'created feelings of terror of constriction in my heart'. His fears were commonplace. Yet large stores were the shape of the future, and it was Associated Dairies (Asda) of Leeds who were to pioneer their development, initially in their northern trading strongholds.

It wasn't as if Leeds was on the other side of the moon from Winsford – merely an hour's drive across the Pennines – but it could just as well have been as far as Grundy was concerned. Convinced that large stores were a temporary aberration, he reported to Tesco House that they would only put 'an economic rope around our necks'. Why he was so dismissive, I can't say. Possibly he was playing down the significance of what was happening in deference to Jack's continuing preference for stores of little more than 4,000 square feet. Or it may have been that in patronizing a comparative newcomer to the retail business he refused to accept that Asda was right, and he was wrong. If so, it would have been in character, for Grundy was never a man to admit to his mistakes.

* * *

We hear a good deal these days about the flexibility of labour, much less of the flexibility of management. Yet the one is as important as the other, for it's nonsensical to pretend that what applies today will apply equally well tomorrow. It won't. In a rapidly changing environment it's impossible to defer the future, as Tesco learned to its cost when Asda began developing large edge-of-town and out-of-town stores. Whatever the reason for Grundy's misjudgement, it was to have punishing consequences as far as Tesco was concerned, for by disguising what was happening in the north, it conditioned the main Board's attitude towards a development that was to revolutionize the whole business of retailing. Tesco, in fact, was being overtaken by the future, as the Board finally came to recognize.

I suppose there are moments in everyone's life that are ineradicable, those fragmentary, but nonetheless vivid, freeze-frames in the mind. One such example began with a phone call from Arthur Thrush: 'Ian, I want you to meet Leslie [Porter] and I out front at

Tesco House by six tomorrow morning'. During the drive north there was no explanation of what we were about, until Arthur said: 'We've decided that you're going to take over at Winsford'. And then, the four of us in Grundy's office, came Leslie's peremptory dismissal: 'Well, Jim, shake hands with your colleagues. I'm sorry to say you're going to retire through ill health, but you can keep your car for a month.'

I drove Leslie and Arthur the few miles to Wilmslow station, and then returned to Winsford where I had the loneliest lunch of my life. Grundy had gone, but the rest of his staff remained, and while I sat by myself at one table in the canteen, they sat at another and watched me; their Nemesis in a lounge suit. For that's what I was. Certainly, it was flattering to be asked to sort out the mess, though I had little idea at the time of what it would entail. Indeed, only one thing was clear: that I would have to begin by re-building the whole of the northern operation from the ground upwards, and to do that would mean calling in my own team to sort out the shambles that I'd inherited. And it was during the next eighteen months, that my chosen executives proved exactly what they were worth to the company.

I'll never forget the first briefing we held in what, until recently, had been Grundy's inner sanctum. As professionals, they could hardly believe what they heard. Which was not altogether surprising. Sometime ago, the 'chaos theory' was in vogue – the idea that a butterfly's flight over Tokyo (or wherever) could trigger a cloudburst in New York – and chaos was what Winsford was about: the domino effect of inadequate management. That was the pass to which Jack's penchant for divide-and-rule had come, and I can still hear Mike Darnell's caustic aside at the end of the session: 'OK, so we've rotated Bronstein and Grundy, but what now?'

It was a 'now' that was to last for the next eighteen months, during which we worked to a punishing schedule to close small and uneconomic stores and develop an embryo, large-store strategy: to eliminate the rotation of stock, and introduce effective control procedures; to establish firm lines of command, and get the message across as to what we were about, and why. Bronstein might have had nothing but contempt for his people, but we knew from the outset that without their co-operation, we would get nowhere at all; that, ultimately, it was our staff who would determine the success or failure of our mission.

The experience was a hellish one, but gradually we got on top of the chaos that was Grundy's legacy and returned Tesco North to profit. Jack, of course, was delighted, though he can hardly have appreciated the irony that one of the key lessons we learned during our time at Winsford was to transform the entire character of Tesco and, at the same time, break his grip on the company.

Traditionally, northerners have always been thrifty shoppers, and it was during our spell in Winsford that it became increasingly clear that Green Shield stamps were passing their sell-by date. By the early 1970s inflation was beginning to bite hard, and as prices rose it focused the public's mind on the diminishing value of the pound in their pockets. Once, when they had never had it so good, Green Shield had provided a cost-free bonus for our customers – that little something extra as they passed through our checkouts. No longer. All the indications were that stamps were becoming increasingly counter-productive, and as real incomes continued to fall, customer resistance towards them continued to grow.

Tesco, in fact, was caught in a double whammy, for while the economics of scale allowed operators, such as Asda, to discount prices in their large stores, Tesco was lumbered with the escalating costs of trading in Green Shield from pocket-handkerchief-sized stores. And the more of the sticky little things we offered, the less attractive they appeared to become. We offered double

stamps, triple stamps, quadruple stamps, and they were junked by
the consumer. We raised the ante – a hundred, two hundred, three
hundred stamps on specified lines – and still they were dumped.
And all this at a cost to the company of £20 million a year, a figure
that has to be multiplied twelve-fold to bring it into line with current prices.

Economics is an arcane discipline, but this was the economics
of madness. Yet Jack still refused to accept the evidence of Tesco's
returns. They weren't to be denied, however, and in 1974 the
company's half-year pre-tax profits showed a 19.8 per cent fall. As
far as the City was concerned Tesco's interim was far worse than
the market was expecting and questions began to be asked about
the company's survival capacity.

The image had some justification, of a reach-me-down
operation trading out of inadequate stores, their windows a Day-
Glo blaze of Green Shield posters. It was out of step with the times.
Tesco was fast becoming a retail anachronism, and by 1975 the
City's fears for its future were reinforced when there was another
sharp fall in the company's profits. Unless something was done,
and quickly, there was a very real prospect that the company
would go to the wall. Today, the idea may appear absurd, but in
the mid-1970s it was a very real possibility. As the situation
deteriorated, it became increasingly obvious that if there was one
thing that could be done to avert the crisis, it was to break the
Green Shield contract, and with it Jack's control of Tesco.

Only those who don't act don't make mistakes. If our mistakes
are obvious in retrospect, however, that's not how it seems at the
time. At the time, there is always the danger that we'll defend our
actions, and in consequence, our mistakes, to the last drop of
someone else's blood. Which, I suspect, is how it was with Jack
Cohen. To him, it may have seemed that large stores were some
kind of retail freak, whilst stamps were the acme of retailing, a

throwback to the days when he peddled compliments to nail down a sale: 'For you, love, two for the price of one, and I can't say fairer than that.' It was all a long time ago, but the old coster-monger remained, and now it was Green Shield that provided the come-on that clinched his sales. Or so he believed. For Jack, they had become a kind of talisman, a measure of his authority as much as his judgement, and I knew that if I was going to challenge either I would have to have irrefutable evidence to support my case. Rationally, the evidence of Tesco's failing performance should have been sufficient to clinch the argument, but then I wasn't dealing with reason, rather with the prejudices of a Board dominated by Jack.

There are no easy options when it comes to taking decisions about people with whom you have worked, and of whom you are fond. Autocrat that he was, Jack nonetheless commanded great affection, a seemingly indestructible presence who, with his king-sized cigar and rusty old voice, had become a caricature of himself. For all the memories of his many kindnesses to me, however, the choice still had to be made – whether the future of the company was of more importance than the man who had made it – and early in 1977 I rang an old friend, Mike O'Connor, then boss of the US Food Marketing Institute, to sound out his views. A no-nonsense character, his reply was much what I expected: 'Hell, Ian, what planet are you living on? Stamps are yesterday's news, which is why so many of our people are dropping them.'

The evidence wasn't conclusive, but it was enough to put before the Board which proceeded to divide against itself, not once, not twice, but innumerable times in the first months of 1977. As the wrangle continued, becoming progressively more acerbic, so the rumours began to circulate. Confidentiality has never been retailing's strong point, and as the in-fighting at Tesco House intensified, so the rumours gained momentum: that Tesco was planning to drop stamps; that Tesco was renegotiating its contract with Green Shield; that Green Shield's boss, Richard Tomkins, was masterminding a new deal that Tesco could not refuse.

Paradoxically, the rumour-mongering had its benefits. In confusing the opposition as to what we were about, it allowed Tesco to disguise its own intentions, and by the spring of 1977 we were actively involved in a campaign of disinformation, which led the retail correspondent of the *Financial Times*, Elinor Goodman, to speculate: 'Few people expect Tesco to abandon stamps altogether. A more likely course of action would be for the company to renegotiate a new contract which would allow it to dispense with stamps in situations where they are seen not to help the trade.'

In part she was right, in part, wrong. Jack was certainly keen to cobble together an agreement with Tomkins, but under the cover of rumour and counter-rumour, we had already test-marketed the impact of offering deep price cuts, in place of stamps, in two of Tesco's smaller Midland stores. Conducted with great secrecy, we even resurrected the trade name Adsega, a small group that had been 'absorbed' by Tesco during Jack's take-over phrase, to disguise what we were about. The evidence was conclusive. It was price cuts, not Green Shield, that our customers wanted, and the deeper our discounts the higher our returns. Yet still the Board couldn't nerve itself to take a decision and, failing that, I was asked to sound out an advertising agency capable of re-launching Tesco – 'just in case', as Leslie Porter explained, 'the vote should go against Green Shield'. Several names were canvassed, and McCann Erickson won the account. Their research was to confirm what we already knew: that at best, the majority of shoppers regarded stamps as handy, at worst as being a positive nuisance.

Combined with our own findings, it was powerful evidence to

deploy in our dealings with the Green Shield negotiating team. What they lacked in detail to refute our case, however, they more than compensated for in the arrogance that led their Chief Executive, Peter Pugsley, to assert that: 'Tesco needs Green Shield more than Green Shield needs Tesco'. And Jack Cohen agreed. For all the cumulative evidence, he was as unwilling to confront reality as he was to quit the contest. That was not his way, and never had been, otherwise Tesco would never have existed. A born fighter, he had spent half a century slugging it out in one of the toughest businesses in the world, and the old fighting spirit still remained. To him, in fact, it must have seemed that this could well be his last stand; that he was fighting not so much for Green Shield as for his life, for Jack, and the company he had created, were inseparable, each an essential part of the other.

The Governor may have been arbitrary, ornery, many things, but no one could question his guts, and he fought every inch of the way against the inevitable: the decision to drop Green Shield stamps.

Not that there was anything inevitable about it when the Board finally met to decide on the matter. Leslie was in the chair, with Jack beside him, a shrunken figure, apparently asleep, but alert to every nuance of the power game that was being played out around him. On a head count he knew that he could rely on 'the family'. As for the rest of us, there was still all to play for, not least, our own futures. Indeed, unless a decision was taken on the future of Tesco, then our own futures were in doubt, for it was no longer possible to go on trading in a half world where no one knew what might happen next. Nothing could be more damaging than that, and on the first vote, I produced a letter from David Behar, an absentee director, who made no bones about where he stood: 'I can't stand the sticky little things. Get rid of them'. I cast his decisive, proxy vote. Momentarily it seemed as if the issue had been settled, but

Jack would have nothing of it, and four more times he demanded a re-count, and four more times he went down to defeat.

For The Governor it was the beginning of the end, for Tesco the end of the beginning, though one final, bizarre act had still to be played out. Tesco's contract with Green Shield was clear – we had to give them one month's notice of our intention to quit stamps – but when we phoned through with the Board's decision, Green Shield's boss, Richard Tomkins, was adamant: 'Your contract still has a year to run'. Seemingly, neither he nor his team had troubled to read through the small print of a contract on which their core business depended. By the evening of 8 May 1977 they had learned the cost of their mistake.

Whatever elation the five of us who voted to end the Green Shield contract may have felt, however, was quickly tempered by the realization of what the decision implied. Some time later, the *Guardian* reported: 'Their [Tesco's] decision was to change the face of Britain's High Streets. The most successful business partnership in post-war Britain was to be severed . . . for Tesco was the supermarket flagship, the jewel in the crown of Green Shield.' That's not how it seemed at the time. It was all very well to drop stamps, and to talk up the benefits of price cutting, but what, in practice, did that mean? True, we had £20 million to re-invest, but the question remained, how best to employ it?

McCann's research provided a partial answer. According to their findings, for all the company's 'friendly market-trader feel', Tesco had a more working-class image than it deserved due, largely, to the clutter in stores, and their gimcrack appearance. As such, the agency came out with two related conclusions: that on price, Tesco's image was better than the reality, whilst on quality, the reality was better than the perceived image. This was the marketing gap that was to provide the platform for the re-launch of Tesco: to refine our image whilst discounting on prices.

So much, however, was more easily said than done. There was little room for refinement in our existing stores. They were too small and ill-planned for that, but in lieu of larger units, we had to do the best with what we had. And this was only half the problem. We might have had a £20 million war chest, but how far would it go, and how long would it last if we launched a major price cutting campaign? For Daisy Hyams, our Buying Director, it posed a nightmarish problem: to compute the profit and loss on a shopping list of 16,000 convenience and durable items, all of which carried their own, carefully calculated margins – and then to do it all over again excluding the Green Shield factor. Ultimately, all depended on Daisy getting her sums right, otherwise we could bankrupt the business.

And all the while, as Daisy permutated her options (a penny off here, tuppence off there), and McCanns planned our media campaign, we were working against the clock. The Green Shield contract ended on 9 May which allowed us only a month to 'pull' stamps from our stores and launch Operation Checkout. McCanns had come up with the slogan, an act of creative brilliance that captured precisely what we were about. If there was any one word that was to provoke customers to test-market for themselves the quality of Tesco's range at prices they could afford it was 'checkout'. Whenever I hear the word, it still gives me a buzz. As the *Daily Mail* reported on 9 May, it seemed as if Tesco was in the process of revolutionizing its business – yet until that morning only a handful of our staff had been privy to the secret. Most of them had heard the rumours, of course, but it wasn't until they read Jack Cohen's statement in the *Sun* – 'Tesco has always done what its customers want. That's why we are going to change our trading policies' – that they learned anything definite about what we were up to. Which, in itself, posed a problem.

Whilst secrecy had been the essence of our strategy until 9

May, the reverse was now the case. The Board could talk until Doomsday, but unless we succeeded in taking our people with us, we might just as well have been talking to ourselves. Indeed, the success or failure of the entire exercise would depend on their collaboration. The old cliché about communications being the essence of good management is all very well in theory. In practice, it is a different matter, the more so when it comes to getting the message across to 35,000 people scattered throughout the country. Yet this is what we were about, and it was this as much as anything else that was to mark Tesco off from its past. An alien notion to Jack Cohen, it was central to our agenda: that from Day One of Operation Checkout, we should open and maintain good lines of communication with our staff.

That afternoon I launched the first phase of what amounted to a communications blitz, at a briefing session for 250 of our top managers. I explained that our objective was three-fold: to increase turnover and market share; to generate and sustain customer loyalty, and to transform Tesco's image and re-position the company in the market. When I finished, they were gobsmacked, as much by what I'd said as by the fact that Tesco House had troubled to take them into its confidence. For as long as most of them could remember, The Governor had practised a culture of secrecy which, during Tesco's times of troubles in the early 1970s, had sapped what little remained of the staff's morale. In fact, our own research had shown how bad the situation had become providing, as it did, a damning indictment of top management as remote, arrogant and tyrannical, all liberally punctuated with four-letter words. In such circumstances, it was not surprising that morale was at rock-bottom, and staff turnover was running at 180 per cent a year. No one, it seemed, had given a damn for their interests, yet now someone was at least bothering to talk to them, and on 10 May, David Malpas and I set off on a 12,000 mile mission to sell-in Operation Checkout to the people in our stores.

And as the countdown continued, so the pace accelerated. On the second floor of Tesco House, Daisy Hyams refined her calculations, while McCanns finalized our media campaign. In late May a small party of us visited the States to see how their retailers had handled the job. It was a lightning foray: Washington, New York, and then Boston where a director of Stop and Shop told us how they had whitewashed the windows of all their stores in the days immediately before dropping stamps: 'OK, so it was gimmicky, but it drove the competition wild just to know what the hell we were about'. Only recently, we had successfully exploited a campaign of disinformation to confuse the opposition. Now we were to whitewash our intentions in the run-in to Operation Checkout.

For public consumption, the date announced for the relaunch was Wednesday, 8 June 1977, three days after the celebrations marking the Silver Jubilee of Queen Elizabeth's accession to the throne. For Tesco's eyes only, the date was set back by twenty-four hours, a critical element in our campaign of planned deception. The ploy was elegant in its simplicity. If we could fool the competition into thinking that we were going to launch Checkout on Wednesday, there was every likelihood that they would mount a pre-emptive strike in an attempt to neutralize our initiative which, in its turn, would allow us a full day in which to fine tune our campaign. And that's exactly what happened.

Over the Jubilee weekend, our staff worked behind whitewashed windows to re-price our stock and re-dress our stores, and on Wednesday, Tesco remained closed for business. It was a high-risk gamble (the loss of a single day's trading in those days amounted to some £2.5 million), but it more than paid off in our subsequent returns. The competition was completely wrong-footed. They reacted before we had even made our move, and it was only at the close of business on Wednesday evening that we released the first of our sixty-second commercials featuring a range of deep price cuts on promoted lines.

As Mike Franklin, the account director from McCanns who masterminded the agency's campaign, was later to say: 'The opposition had expected Tesco to go on the 8th. As it was, they were left competing against themselves without any idea of what Tesco was going to do. In effect, they were price cutting against an unknown quantity, and this gave Tesco a terrific advantage.' It was an under-statement that was dwarfed by events, but when David Malpas and I met in my office for a drink that Wednesday evening the best we could do was to toast our luck: 'Here's to Checkout, or we won't be here this time next week'.

Not that we had that long to wait. By lunchtime on Thursday, the switchboard at Tesco House was being swamped with calls from stores all over the country: from High Wycombe, where a twenty-five yard queue had formed before the store had even opened for business; from Pontypridd, where the crowds were so large that the manager had been forced to close the doors; from Swansea and Crawley where customers were emptying the trolleys of staff trying to refill the shelves: from Preston, where turnover had increased by 200 per cent, and the store was running out of supplies. Quite literally, Tesco was being overwhelmed by demand. The only question that remained was: Would it hold up?

By the weekend, we had the answer. Once begun, it seemed as if the buying mania was developing a momentum of its own, and many of our stores were in a state of virtual siege. As the *Sun* reported, this was 'High Noon on the High Street'. They were not the only ones to be intrigued by the story. In fact, it was subsequently estimated that the free publicity we achieved for Checkout was worth some £5 million. And all the while, the competition could only watch and wonder how long the demand would hold up, for as one City broker reflected: 'It is one thing to persuade customers to purchase well advertised, heavily price-cut special items. It is another to convince them to change their shopping patterns, yet this is exactly what Tesco has to do to achieve a sharp improvement in profit growth'.

They could not have summarized our objectives better. Immediately, Checkout had provided us with the lift-off to re-position Tesco. Now our aim was to 'take the tiger by the tail' and exploit what we had achieved. And The Governor was quick to claim the credit for both. Of course, he had had growing doubts about Green Shield. Of course, he had been all in favour of Checkout. Of course, we had to build for the future. The old auto-crat was incorrigible as ever, though he was little more than a husk of the man whom I had first met at the Grand Hotel in Eastbourne almost twenty years before. The chutzpah remained, but little else. A sick man, he was dying piecemeal, though when I saw him in hospital early in 1979, there was no disguising his enthusiasm at the prospect of a visit to one of the new range of Tesco's large stores.

It was early in March when I got a call from Jack's chauffeur: 'Sir John's planning to go to Pitsea today'. I managed to get there before him, and the manager and I were waiting when his Rolls arrived. Between us, we managed to get him into his wheelchair, and within minutes of pushing him into the store he was sur-rounded by a crowd of well-wishers. Essex has always been a colony for the migrants of London's East End, and it seemed as if half of them were there to shake Jack's hand, and share their memories of the-time-that-was with him: 'I'll never forget . . .', 'My mum always said . . .', 'Course, the old place is gone now . . .'

At lunchtime we went up to the manager's office where Jack had his favourite snack – a smoked salmon sandwich and a glass of Scotch – and when he finished, he asked if I would push him out on to the balcony overlooking the shop floor. How long we were there, I can't say. All that I do know is that when I finally turned to him, there were tears rolling down his cheeks, and I said, 'Are you alright, Governor?' and almost inaudibly he replied: 'I never imagined that this was how it would be'. Just that. Nothing more, and we took him down to the car, and he waved as it pulled away. The following day, The Governor died.

CHAPTER THREE

Tesco: The Thinking Retailer

There had been a time when the idea would have seemed absurd. But it was not only the kudos we welcomed, more the growing recognition by local authorities that we were no longer the cowboys who had once ridden roughshod through Britain's High Streets.

THERE IS A bit of a dynast in all of us, and that was certainly true of Jack Cohen. So much, I suppose, was inevitable. There is a Yiddish conundrum which asks: 'If I am only for myself, what am I?', and for all his taste for power, I suspect that the answer Jack ultimately came to was that there was more to him than the wheeler-dealer who had never done business by sitting on his arse; that he did, indeed, have something to hand on to the future, if only the perpetuation of his own hegemony. Which was appreciable. For almost half a century he had devoted himself to Tesco, often at the expense of his family. Now it was his family – or more precisely, Shirley Porter – who were to inherit his chutzpah, if not his empire.

In many ways they were very similar, Jack and his daughter Shirley. Ambitious and ruthless, they made dangerous enemies – though none more dangerous than to themselves! The difference was that where Jack had earned his authority, Shirley believed that her standing in the Tesco hierarchy was hers by rights. When

Checkout was launched, however, we had more to think about than the perpetuation of the Cohen dynasty. Nothing, it is said, fails like success, but if in general the condition breeds complacency, the reverse was true in Tesco's case. It wasn't that we were complacent about what we had achieved, rather about coping with our success.

When I was young there was a vogue for jigsaws, massive things, impenetrable, and I'd wonder how so many odd-shaped pieces could ever be fitted together to make the picture on the lid of the box. That was very much how it was at Tesco in 1977. We may have succeeded in demolishing the old puzzle, but the question remained: What should we put in its place? How could we create a rational framework that would allow us to realize the picture which existed, if only in our mind's eye? It was all very well to say: 'We're going to become the M&S of the food business', and to laugh at our own presumption, but if that was our objective, then where should we begin?

Ironically, it was Jack who provided the answer: with people. He may have lost touch with the 1970s, but during his heyday his slogan about 'piling it high and selling it cheap' was an exact reflection of the public's mood. At a time when a thousand-a-year man was looked upon as someone who had made good, shopping for luxuries was something that few could afford. Growing affluence, and the consumer revolution, had changed all that. Nonetheless, people were still our business. All too often, the service industries are inclined to forget this, more especially in the financial sector where banks still look at their customers, and rather than saying: 'How can I help them? How can I make their life easier?', tend to say: 'How much money can we make out of them?'.

Banks still have a long way to go before they live up to their user-friendly image. Which was the lesson that Tesco had to relearn in 1977, a lesson that Jack had never forgotten: that it was our customers who would deliver the final verdict on Checkout, and with it, on the future of the company. Momentarily, we were euphoric – and who wouldn't have been as turnover went through the roof? – but it was short-lived, for the miracle was that Tesco survived its own success. Indeed, I can remember wondering whether that retail analyst had not been right when he had doubted if the company would be able to capitalize on what it achieved.

He wasn't alone with his reservations. There were plenty of sceptics who shared his doubts, not least, in the City, but my team at Tesco House would have nothing of their jeremiads. After all, they had heard it all before, the chorus of doomwatchers who had so often in the past written off Tesco as 'the company with the great future behind it'. Here they were again. This time, however, it was different. This time they were talking-down the evidence of Tesco's success provided – and the provisos multiplied like rabbits in the post-Checkout days – we could rationalize a distribution system that was close to breaking point due to a 40 per cent increase in turnover; provided the staff in our stores could cope with the pressure of demand; and above all else, provided we had the nerve to invest in our success.

Our determination to 'think long', however, was something that the City failed to understand, which was not altogether surprising. Traditionally, the majority of City institutions have been what a former Chancellor called 'crash ball players', looking for a quick return on their capital, careless of the damage that this has inflicted in the UK economy. The condition is innate, yet how can any company hope to plan sensibly for the future, when operating to such abbreviated financial deadlines? How is it possible for them to re-gear or re-position themselves in the market when operating under such tight, financial constraints? Which, in part, is why, in the years immediately after the launch of Checkout, the markets continued to write the company down, failing to appreciate that the increased income being generated by the company was being re-invested so that Tesco would live up to the image we had visualized for it.

In one, paradoxical respect, however, the City's doubts about Tesco's performance may have proved its salvation in disguise. To this day, I've never been able to explain why the company wasn't the subject of a takeover bid, more especially, from British American Tobacco, the owners of International Stores. When we finally announced that we were going to drop stamps, International snapped up the Green Shield franchise, with punishing consequences. Perhaps they thought they could capitalize on our decision, but when the media started to carry stories contrasting Tesco and International price lists, they realized the extent of their mistake. While our business burgeoned, their's nose-dived – which is when the doomwatchers saved us. At a time when they had virtually written Tesco off, BAT could have snapped Tesco up. That they didn't has always surprised me. Possibly, British American weren't really interested in retailing, but whatever their reason, their failure provided us with the breathing space to get on with the job of re-structuring the company and revamping its image.

But while image is important, it is by no means everything. You can 'spin' an image as much as you like, but unless the message has substance, it will soon be exposed for what it is: illusory. In trying to fool the people there is always the risk that you'll fool yourself at the same time. Not that that was the case when David Malpas, Mike Darnell, and the rest of us met to formulate a development strategy for Tesco. There was no prospect of fooling ourselves when confronted with the realities of the inadequacy of the size and design of our stores; of the deficiencies of our warehousing and merchandising operations; of the eccentricities (and that's to put it mildly) of our control systems.

At first glance, the problems were so numerous and complex as to appear insuperable. Unless they could be rectified, however, there wasn't any hope of realizing our ambitions of re-making the company. Indeed, one of the first questions we had to ask ourselves was if the name 'Tesco' had become a liability. Smacking, as it did, of a long time past when Jack bought out the London tea importers T. E. Stockwell, to merge the title with that of the Cohens and thus create the company name Tesco, would it not be better to drop the name and begin all over again? Even before we came out of stamps, the question had racked the Board, and it was Mike Franklin's team who provided us with the answer: that we should stick with the name, just as long as we could improve the company's image.

My own children know nothing of the Tesco-that-was, but there are still lots of people who remember its not-so-distant past. In fact, this change of perception has been central to the company's success, for customer profiles now show that more young people shop with Tesco than with any other retailer in the UK, whilst older people continue to favour Sainsbury's. I can't imagine that this generation gap is something that troubles the present Tesco Board. The past may be a good place to visit, but it is no place to stay, and that was certainly true as far as 1977 was concerned. Then it was all very well to 'think long', but that was to trade in abstractions, and following the launch of Checkout we had little time for such indulgences.

* * *

Oscar Wilde once remarked that philosophy teaches us to bear with equanimity the misfortunes of our neighbours. In 1977, we had problems enough of our own without worrying about other people's, not least how to tackle our distribution crisis. In our wildest dreams we'd never imagined that Checkout would generate such an astronomic lift-off in sales, but without being able to get supplies into our stores in sufficient quantities to meet demand, there was a very real danger that we'd become the laughing stock of the trade for promoting cuts that we couldn't deliver.

Pre-Checkout, 85 per cent of our stock had come straight to our stores from the company's suppliers, and the bottlenecks this caused in the immediate post-Checkout period were horrendous. Indeed, the tales of those times have become a staple of the Checkout legend: of our four, obsolescent warehouses working all hours, and then asking for more; of the vehicles at any one of our 900 stores that were handling up to 120 separate deliveries a week, all of which had to be unloaded by hand and then humped up one, or even two floors to our storerooms. This was testing us to breaking point, and it made a mockery of all that we were trying to achieve. In short, unless it was possible to rationalize the system, then there was little likelihood that we would be able to capitalize on the gains we had achieved. We did have the tiger by the tail, but the question remained: Who was taming whom?

As far as our immediate problem was concerned, the answer lay in opening new warehouses that would help us to centralize our distribution system and, in the process, eliminate the practice of our suppliers delivering directly to the stores. Within eighteen months of the launch of Checkout, we had added 400,000 square feet of warehousing to our existing facilities, and as each new unit came on line, the bottlenecks were progressively reduced – from 120 weekly deliveries, to 80, then 60, and downwards to a point where, today, the company's 560 large stores receive only a handful of deliveries each week, and 95 per cent of their supplies come directly from Tesco's own depots.

So much, of course, is the kind of throw-away statistic that is easily shrugged off, yet it's one which disguises the reality not only of what was involved, but also of what it entailed. Ultimately, strategy is all about making connections, of connecting up the pieces so they form part of the whole. The re-structuring of our distribution network complemented, exactly, the development of our large store programme. Indeed, the one without the other would have negated the function of both.

In this respect, we were fortunate. Even before the launch of Checkout, the Board had finally nerved itself to invest in a large store programme, though this was easier said than done. As early as 1975, a former President of the Royal Town Planning Institute, Ewart Parkinson, had provided us with a damning indictment of the attitude of local planning authorities to the company. Quite simply, they didn't want 'cowboys' like Tesco on their patch. They had had more than enough of our wheeler-dealings for planning consents in the past. And now that unwanted past had caught up with us. Without being able to convince local councils that we were, indeed, changing our ways, we would be stuck with the small and pokey stores that made nonsense of our ambitions to reinvent the company.

Not that Tesco was alone with the problem. For the majority of town planners, and the councils they represented, the concept of large stores had become problematic, partly because retailers had made little, if any, constructive effort to explain what they were about. It was this communications gap that we aimed to fill. Our objective was straightforward: to open, and maintain a dialogue with local authorities to explain the thinking behind large stores, and to indicate that Tesco was trying to think through the manifold problems that were of concern to both retailers and planners – of the effect of social and economic change on people's lifestyles, of the implications of globalization for the food chain, of the impact of information technology on employment structures. In essence, of trying to take the future by the tail!

This was strong stuff for a company which, historically, had never appeared to consider tomorrow, as long as it turned a profit today. Initially, the launch of what we termed our Occasional Papers was greeted with a good deal of derision: 'What was Tesco on about?' 'How could it presume on the future when it had had such a razzamatazz past?' The scenario just didn't add up, yet four years, and half a dozen Occasional Papers later, we were being invited to submit papers to the Long Range Planning Society, and being described in a leading trade journal as 'the thinking retailer'.

Tesco, the thinking retailer! There had been a time when the idea would have seemed absurd. But it was not only the kudos we welcomed, more the growing recognition by local authorities that we were no longer the cowboys who had once ridden roughshod through Britain's High Streets. While theorizing about the future was all very well in principle, it was left to our Estates Director, Francis Krejsa, to turn out theories into practice. A quiet-spoken man, whose diffidence disguised one of the best brains in the estates business, Francis was later to say that before Checkout, the only plan that Tesco subscribed to was cutting as many corners as possible, whilst post-Checkout we had a clear idea of the sort of stores we needed – single storey units with flat car parks.

For all our efforts to open a dialogue with local authorities, nonetheless a good deal of resistance remained during the early days of our large-store development programme. Expunging Tesco's past was not as easy as all that. Our reputation remained to haunt us which was why, whenever we won a planning consent on appeal, we would always go back to the local authority concerned and say: 'Look, what kind of store would you like?', and work as closely as possible with them to provide the sort of development they wanted. It was a painstaking business, but essential, for the whole, future image of the company depended on it. Slowly, but surely, our investment in dialogue paid off. In 1979 our development budget exceeded £10 million for the first time, a figure that was to pale into insignificance during the 1980s and into the 1990s, when we were opening an average of 25 large stores a year, many at a cost of more than £15 million.

I know that some people still have reservations about such developments. Like everything else in life, however, retailing can't stand still. That has never been its way. It has always evolved from market stall to corner shop, from piling it high and selling it cheap, to taking the waiting out of wanting, and the more rapid the social and economic changes, the more rapidly retailers have had to adapt to survive in what is, arguably, the most competitive business in the world. The alternative, as Tesco nearly discovered, is to get locked into the past, and become an endangered species.

Yet, while change is inherent, the past has an uncanny knack of repeating itself. In the post-Checkout period, it became increasingly clear to us that if Tesco was to become the M&S of the food business, then we would have to rationalize the whole range of our merchandise which, in turn, would mean abandoning our investment in home n'wear. Besides creating a conflict of image, there simply wasn't sufficient room in our existing stores to handle both lines if our ambitions were to be realized. It was a tough decision for Leslie Porter, our Chairman, to take. As Jack's son-in-law and, thus, 'one of the family', he had joined the Board from Harrow Stores specifically to handle Tesco's venture into the home n'wear market, but he was quick to accept the rationale of my team as he was to support us in our efforts to reposition the company.

Albeit a bit of a wheeler-dealer, Leslie was an ebullient and amiable character – except, that is, when Shirley had been having a go at him about the way we were running the business – and even though I was his second choice as Tesco's Managing Director, we always got on well together. In the wrangling of the early 1970s, the post had been divided between myself, on the retail side, and Laurie Leigh, a close friend of Leslie's, on home 'n' wear. In 1974, however, Laurie had a heart attack, and died while travelling back from Winsford, leaving me as Leslie's sole MD. I don't place much credence in fate, but if Laurie had lived, the story of Tesco could well have been different. As it was, all I could say to Leslie was: 'Look, this is a terrible thing that's happened, and I'm sure you would rather have lost me than Laurie, but I'll give you the best that I've got'.

And I did, though what Laurie would have made of Leslie's backing for our decision to drop home n'wear, I can't say. All I do know is that when David Malpas produced the first results of the trials to rationalize our merchandise, there could be no further questions about the validity of our decision. Where, previously, our existing stores had been a hotch-potch of lines – canned goods flanked by racks of clothing; groceries competing for space with white goods – they were now able to concentrate their attention on achieving our objective of becoming Britain's No. 1 food retailer. Which, in its turn, posed a problem and provided us with an insight into the business itself.

As for the problem, it was all very well for us to talk-up quality when that was just what so many of our lines lacked. The whole quality control process remained primitive. Indeed, unless we could improve the standard of our products, there was a very real danger that we'd fall victim to the practice of 'Selling the sizzle, and not the steak', which was why, as Francis was negotiating for planning consents, and David was restructuring our merchandising strategy, we made the first moves towards establishing a high-tech department responsible for ensuring that all the goods we sold carried our own seal of approval.

A crucial initiative, it was to play a significant role in helping transform Tesco's image – and not only that of Tesco. Within six years of the launch of Checkout, we took on the government itself when we launched our Healthy Eating Campaign. Of course, there had been food fads before – most notably during the 1920s when 'the balanced diet' became *de rigueur* for those who were able to afford it – but this was something quite different. During the 1970s, there had been growing concern about the impact of the nation's eating habits on people's health. And the more penetrating the questions, the more opaque the replies. At times, in fact, it seemed that the whole industry (producers, manufacturers, retailers) were engaged in a conspiracy of silence orchestrated by the Ministry of Agriculture, Food and Fisheries.

Matters came to a head in 1983. For a couple of years, the National Advisory Committee on Nutrition Education had been studying the whole, complex question of diet, and it was rumoured that their final report could well be suppressed. Apparently, powerful interests were at work that were determined to restrict the public's right to know what they were eating. And to disguise their intentions, the industry and its agents in Whitehall dissembled. It was not that people did not have the right to know, rather that food labelling was a fiendishly complicated business. Just what should be included on such labels if they were to be meaningful? Just how much could the public be expected to understand if items were labelled? A self-fulfilling catechism, it served everyone's interests except that of the consumer – and in January 1985, David Malpas put an end to the farce when he launched Tesco's Healthy Eating Campaign. As he was to say at the time:

> We're pretty big people in the food business, and what we hope to do is to influence other manufacturers to follow our lead by

saying, 'Look, we are putting more information on our own packs' so that the whole industry does it, and not just have it as a Tesco initiative.

Once, such an initiative would have been laughed off, but this time it was underwritten by Tesco's growing expertise. In little more than half a decade, and backed by the resources of our food technology division, the company was not only well on the way to realizing its commitment to quality control, but was also sufficiently confident to lead where others were to follow, for *The Times* was to write later: 'The emphasis which Tesco is to place on the environmental qualities of its produce will make the mass market inescapably conscious of the cause'.

As for the insight, the more closely we examined the whole question of merchandising, the more evident it became that there was no such thing as 'public taste'. It may be a convenient notion, but nonetheless it's a myth. However hard marketing gurus try to sell-in the idea that taste can be packaged, peddled and homogenized – the consumer consumerized – the general public are too independent-minded, too ornery for that. They know what they like, and like what they know, and wide variations persist as much in regional as in personal taste. To which, all I can say is *vive la différence!*, though the full extent of that difference only became clear when we analysed our merchandising strategy. Where, previously, we had traded on the assumption that what sold in Sunderland would go down equally well in Southend, that our consumers in southern England, concerned with healthy eating, shared a sweet-tooth in common with the Scots, we now had to revise our thinking, and gear our merchandising to satisfy local demand.

Not that this shift in perception of our customers and of ourselves happened overnight. Throughout the early 1980s, Tesco was on a steep learning curve, but there could be no disguising Francis Krejsa's delight when he announced to the Board, in 1987, that M&S had agreed to work with Tesco on the first of a series of joint development projects. Exactly ten years had passed since my team had sat down to decide how to reinvent Tesco, for the doomwatchers to mock our ambition: the M&S of the food business, indeed! Seemingly, we were to have the last laugh.

Nonetheless, the ironies remain, for a decade later, and with space to spare in its modern stores, Tesco is now back into home n'wear. As I've said, the past has an uncanny habit of repeating itself, the more so since Tesco decided to declare a price war on certain of its major suppliers in 1996.

Jack Cohen would have revelled in Tesco's contest with suppliers such as Levi Strauss, Calvin Klein, and Nike. Make no mistake about it, the mark-up on certain brand names is so disproportionately high that even allowing for our own deep price cuts, Tesco continues to make a profit on their sales.

* * *

If any one factor accounted for the quiet revolution that transformed Tesco, it was the application of advanced systems. We have specialists in this, and specialists in that, and specialists in the other, but the ultimate specialist is the character who can work the advanced systems that determine what all the rest of us specialists will do. Or, rather, how their mysteries can be turned to good account, as they were with Operation Checkout.

I don't place much credence in coincidence, but there can be no question that the launch of Checkout was largely powered by the coincidental introduction of the Electronic Point Of Sale (EPOS) system. Until the mid-1970s, virtually every item going through our stores had to be price-marked, a time-consuming, labour-intensive and high-cost operation. The arrival of EPOS was to change all that. We no longer had to price-mark our products, and by automatically recording the turnover in our stores, the EPOS system provided instant feedback of information to head office, thus allowing us to place orders directly with our suppliers, who could then deliver straight into our warehouses. As increasingly sophisticated systems have come on-line, it sometimes seems as if the process is inexorable, as if advanced systems are developing an intelligence of their own. The prospect is mind boggling. Of course, it's all too easy to make a bogey of what we don't understand, and heaven knows, the mysteries of modern technology are beyond most people's comprehension, which places an enormous responsibility on its agents: a point that Donald Harris, who masterminded our information technology programme during the 1970s, never tired of repeating. In fact, I still have a copy of a document – another of the Occasional Papers series – which Donald delivered to Euro MPs in Strasbourg in 1981:

> Increasingly, our problems turn on the management of information, on handling the extraordinary mass of computerized data carried by the volume business that is retailing today . . . In fact, multiples now trade as much in data as in goods, and if data is power, then it imposes a heavy responsibility on those who manage it to ensure that it is used for responsible ends.

Platitudes are easy enough to peddle, though Donald's strictures were nothing new, rather the conundrum of progress itself. I suppose that it is a problem that we have always had to live with since some Stone Age whizz-kid first fashioned an axe, and wondered what to use it for: to attack the opposition, or to chop sticks for the fire? Indeed, this has always been the dilemma of progress, the ends to which technological advances will be used – and the more rapid the advances, the more pressing the need for the answers become.

Which, I suspect, was the essence of Donald's concern of twenty years ago – a concern that has added force today, not least in the contentious field of data protection. In the process of assembling data, it is inevitable that companies, such as Tesco, accumulate a vast amount of information about the habits and tastes of their customers, and in consequence, about their lifestyles which, in turn, allows them to tailor their supply to consumer demand. As always, however, there is a downside to such advances: the danger that companies will exploit such information for their own, unscrupulous ends, which is why Tesco was an early signatory to the 1984 Data Protection Act.

Ultimately, of course, it is impossible to legislate for the responsibility any more of companies than of individuals, though there could be no questions about Tesco's intentions when it established the Gateshead Project in the early 1980s. As the first of its kind, though still absent from the *Guinness Book of Records*, the scheme was designed to provide disadvantaged people – more especially the old, the handicapped, and single parent families – with interactive shopping facilities via terminals established in their local libraries and community centres. Elegant in its simplicity, the programme allowed customers to dial-up Tesco's 'shopping lists' (which included comparative information on prices and nutrient values), to key in their orders, which were then delivered to their homes. Devised and implemented by Dr Ross Davies, in association with local social services departments, it was the shape of things that have still to come, for while interactive shopping is now the buzzword of retailing, its full potential has yet to be realized.

But then few people are able to grasp the full potential of advanced systems, or appreciate how quickly they have evolved.

Indeed, I find it as challenging as it is impressive that if it took at least a millennium to develop the abacus, and a century to perfect the cash register, then it has taken little more than a quarter of a century for the microchip to transform the whole shape of our lives. Sometimes, in fact, I feel that time itself is being foreshortened. The full implications of what that entails have yet to be explored, of whether it is yet another and intensified case of technological lead and social lag.

All that I do know is that without the technological means to reinvent Tesco, it is doubtful whether the company would have survived. Here again, however, was the paradox that at the final reckoning, Jack Cohen was right. It is not so much computers as *people* that our business is about. For all the skills of the marketing boffins, for all the potential of advanced systems, there is no more possibility of homogenizing taste than there is of dehumanizing people.

Yet even before the advent of EPOS, many of our staff felt, if not dehumanized, then irrelevant. And the problem started at the top. It was all very well for us, the bosses, to indulge in our grand designs for the future – of developing new, large stores; of rationalizing the company's merchandising strategy; of introducing new, smart systems – but unless we could take our staff along with us, we might just as well have kept our fantasies to ourselves. For that's what they would have amounted to, fantasies, without being able to mobilize the energy of our workforce: the 35,000 men and women who, in those days, were in the front-line of Operation Checkout.

During my time as Chairman of Tesco, I was constantly being asked: 'How do you create and motivate a team?' It is the $64,000 question, and I am afraid to say that all too often I would look a bit shifty, and then permutate my reply: 'Well, you see, it's either this, or . . .', all the while wondering at what I was hearing, for the answer is more than a matter of soundbites. Indeed, the subject is one of those riddles wrapped in an enigma of which Churchill was so fond, for there is no explaining the chemistry of good management. Like moonshine, it defies exact definition.

* * *

Too long ago for comfort, I captained my school football and cricket XIs, which was where I learned most of what I know about team building. Teenagers don't take kindly to being pushed around. They are too self-assured for that. Either they are for you or against you which, I suppose, is what team building is all about: getting on with people so they feel that you are on their side, and not some sort of pop-up ego who chanced to be where they are by happenstance. And when my team took the field to kick Checkout about, that was the essence of our game plan. Even then, however, some of us still had to learn that there was more to the game than the individual skills we contributed to it, that for all the expertise we brought into play, Tesco was staffed by people much like ourselves.

Arrogance is the eighth deadly sin – as deadly, that is, to the arrogant as it is to those they patronize. Sainsbury's patronized Tesco when the company launched its Clubcard – and paid the price for their arrogance in the months that followed. Shirley Porter's arrogance was, at the close, to cost her much more than a place on Tesco's Board – as she has time to consider in her self-imposed exile. And the arrogance of Tesco management – of the Them and Us syndrome – was a consistent feature of the research we commissioned in the mid- and late-1970s. Not that there were any grounds for our conceit. Like myself, most of the Tesco House team had had to work their way up through the company, yet there it was, in McKinseys' words: 'In conclusion, we have found that a high proportion of Tesco staff regard the company's senior management as, at best, remote and arrogant, at worst, dictatorial.'

The indictment was a damning one: that in the course of making a success of our own careers, we had neglected the fact that we, too, had started out on the shop floor. Maybe our workforce had not been so fortunate in the game-play of life, but like David Malpas, Mike Darnell, and the rest of us, they, too, had their problems and worries: worries about their mortgages, their families, and their futures; worries, in short, about the thousand-and-one problems that can make a nightmare of our everyday lives. In this respect, no one is unique.

*   *   *

Looking back now, it is easy enough to identify the mistakes that I made during my time at Tesco, of the times that I said to Ann: 'Sorry, dear, you'll have to take care of that. I've got this or that or the other to do'; of the times I bought off my conscience by slipping my children a fiver with the plea: 'You know how it is, work calls. Maybe we'll make it next weekend . . .' Or the next, or the one after that, until the excuses became threadbare, and then it was too late for amends. For all the pressures of success, there can be no rationalizing away such neglect, all of which was in the name of what? My own self-interest, or that of Tesco? There could be no divorcing the one from the other. For half my life I lived Tesco, and the more I succeeded, the more distant my family seemed to become, until a day arrived when my son, Neil, turned on me and remarked bitterly: 'D'you know something, to most people I don't exist, except as Ian MacLaurin's son.'

I've always suspected that living in the shadow of what many people regard as success must be hard. Now I know it. The perks of office are all very well, provided they are not secured at other people's cost: at the cost of my children to whom I was all-too-often an absentee parent when they were growing up; at the cost of my wife, who was left to handle all those thousand-and-one problems of making a home for myself and the children. Only that is not how it should have been. Whatever my success, I should have known better than to regard my family as 'Any Other Business' on the agenda of life. Certainly, they have benefited, materially, from what success I have had, but I am still left wondering whether that compensates for what such success has involved.

Of course, it is too late now to have regrets for past mistakes, but there's always the niggling 'if only . . .' doubt, but then that's to play happenstance with the past which is something that I've always regarded as pointless, and which my team certainly had no time for when it came to repositioning Tesco. Quite the opposite. Our goal was to expunge the past and, in the process, establish a new relationship between Them and Us. In fact, top management as much as the staff were on a long learning curve, each trying to understand what the other was about, for while we knew precisely where we wanted to go, the critical factor was to enlist their support in getting there.

During her time in office, Mrs Thatcher talked a great deal about the 'trickle down' effect, but in my book the 'trickle up' effect is equally important. Indeed, good management is a two-way trade, for to be effective, top-down management needs to generate a positive, bottom-up response. And as far as Tesco was concerned, that took time to achieve, and this at a time when we were trying to transform the company's public image as much as its internal culture. In essence, the two are indistinguishable, for it's the person on the checkout desk who is the public face of Tesco. Of course, that's always been the case since Jack Cohen had first joshed his customers in Well Street market, and I had pattered-on about getting the butter from a non-existent fridge around the back of our Neasden store, and just occasionally in the post-Checkout period I'd play the game of Now and Then, and surprise myself with the enormity of change.

And as the pace of change accelerated, so the need to provide our staff with the skills necessary to run the new business that we were trying to create intensified. And not only that. Of equal importance, there was a need to convince them that we were not the despots they had once believed. Certainly, there were practical measures that we could adopt, a compendium of personnel relations – the introduction of trainee programmes, the establishment of a share option and pension schemes, the provision of in-store canteens and rest rooms. Ultimately, however, all would depend on our recognition that Tesco was only as good as the people with whom we worked. In the process of reinventing the company, in fact, it seemed, at times, as if we were reinventing ourselves, or rather rediscovering what Jack had always been fond of preaching: that the most important person in the business is the character at the bottom of the pile.

And as Tesco's success took off, our confidence burgeoned, and with it the morale of our staff. I've always believed that confidence is infectious, a communicable thing. Either it is there, or it's not, and when Mike Atherton led the lads out on to the Barbados Oval on the fourth day of the '98 Test against the West Indies with a 375 run lead, it seemed to me that they were walking ten feet tall. Only a couple of days before they were being written-off as has-beens, but now there could be no holding them – until rain stopped play. And as I sat there in the pavilion and watched the storm clouds drive across the ground, I thought that that was very much how it had been with Tesco. Where, for so long, the staff had been on the losing side, and morale was at rock bottom, they had now taken an innings lead over the opposition, and with it had recovered their confidence not only in Tesco but in themselves. Then Phil Tufnell said: 'We was robbed', and I was back in the post-Checkout days.

Nonetheless, the conviction holds good: confidence *is* communicable. Balance sheets are all very well as far as they go, but they don't go far enough. Desiccated things, they tend to disguise the fact that staff morale has a direct impact on a company's relationship with its customers who are the bottom-line of every P&L account. And in the case of retailers like Tesco, this is very much an immediate and hands-on affair. Consumer 'profiles' can tell us just so much, but there is more to their preferences than can ever be revealed on a computer print-out – all those small, often idiosyncratic, and highly personal reasons that account for where people shop, and why.

In the immediate post-Checkout period, of course, the answer was clear, for price is the measure of all things during a period of runaway inflation. However, an equally pressing question remained: How could we consolidate on our success and convince the doomwatchers that the operation was not simply a flash-in-the-pan? No question, we were generating increased turnover, and no question, either, that we were investing heavily in the future of the company. At the final reckoning, however, it would be our customers who would determine whether they would continue to 'shop Tesco', which is why, in the early 1980s, we established the first of our Consumer Panels.

Today it may not sound like a significant initiative. Then it was a groundbreaking investment, yet another recognition of the need to adopt a bottom-up approach, this time by obtaining positive feedback from our customers. Which is critical. Once, it was possible to trade in hard-sell, an art form of which Jack Cohen was a past master: 'To hell with the quality, just feel the width!' Those days have long gone. Today's customers are too well informed, too discerning to be taken in by hype. The media have seen to that.

If your products don't live up to the standards your customers expect, they very quickly rumble you.

And it was Tesco's Consumer Panels who played, and continue to play, a key role in helping to create this interface between supply and demand. Originally there were only a handful of them. Now they operate throughout the UK. Small groups of shoppers recruited at random, they meet with Tesco's regional managers and head office staff on a regular basis to discuss their shopping experiences at Sainsbury's, or Harrods, or at the place-round-the-corner, or wherever they may happen to shop. A small initiative, possibly, but an invaluable one not so much for the 'profile' which the Panels provide of changing consumer tastes, more for the shopper's-eye-view they provide of what the competition is doing, and why, which enables Tesco to identify where the company's going wrong, and what can be done about it.

In fact, it was as a direct result of comments from our Panels that Tesco launched its Clubcard scheme in 1996. 'OK,' they said, 'so we're loyal to Tesco, so why not show us a bit of loyalty in return? Why don't you have something like an Air Miles scheme so we can collect points when we shop with you?' And they were right, which was why, after examining the idea, Tesco launched its Clubcard. Currently, there are some ten million card holders which says something for the loyalty factor involved and, which, coincidentally, provides Tesco with invaluable, back-up information about what's going on in the minds of its customers.

But then Tesco in the late 1990s is a far cry from what it had been when we first took the tiger by the tail, for the Jeremiahs to dismiss our hopes of reinventing the company as so much hype. Not that it took them all that long to realize the extent of their mistake. As little as eighteen months after the launch of Checkout, David Churchill, then the retail correspondent of the *Financial Times*, was writing:

Checkout was the acid test of a new breed of management. No one really believed that Tesco was capable of acting so consistently, and so forcibly, and this scepticism goes a long way to explain the dilatory response by other retailers to the Tesco initiative. Quite simply, they thought that the company was going to kill itself, and just hung around to see when that would happen.

And in this, they weren't alone. The markets were equally sceptical, until our investment programme began to generate its own returns. Then it was different. Then they were all gung-ho for Tesco. And as the pieces in our jigsaw fell into place, and our profits doubled and then re-doubled, the financial wiseacres were as quick to forget their former pessimism as they were keen to talk-up the Tesco miracle. Apparently, the company could do no wrong, and when I succeeded Leslie Porter as Tesco Chairman at the AGM in 1985, I wondered, briefly, what Jack would have made of it all – before a lady in the audience rose to nominate Shirley Porter for a seat on the Board.

CHAPTER FOUR

Oh, Lady Porter!

Everything had been going smoothly, and the transfer of power
had been agreed, when a lady rose to propose Shirley as a non-
executive director. Quick as a flash, she obtained a seconder, to
the consternation of the Board.

AT TIMES I feel sorry for Shirley Porter. Not often, of course. Very
rarely, in fact. But on the odd occasions when I'm feeling
generous to a woman who tried to make a hell of my life at Tesco,
I recognize how hard it must have been for her to be Jack Cohen's
daughter, and what an impossible act she was attempting to follow. Possibly she never grasped the fact that her father was a one-
off, or possibly she simply fooled herself into believing that she
had the makings of his successor. Whatever the case, all that I
know is that she was obsessed with power, a sorcerer's apprentice
who brewed-up the concoction that eventually destroyed her.
Which was her tragedy: that she learned everything from Jack
including the ability never to accept that she could be wrong.

As soon as Leslie Porter became Chairman of Tesco, she began
trying to meddle in the business and, in the process, made his life,
and ours a hell. Monday was his worst day, after he had spent a
weekend at home. Normally, the most easy-going and affable of
characters, he would arrive at the office like a bear with a sore
head, and grumble his way through to lunchtime, by which time

he had finally recovered from the shock of being over-exposed to Shirley's strictures. In the interim, however, it seemed that nothing was right at Tesco, that the company was going downhill, whilst if only we'd . . .

. . . and there was Shirley, a shadowy but inescapable presence in our midst. Or not so shadowy, as the case may be. As Leslie's No. 2, Ann and I were often invited to attend functions together with Shirley and Leslie. It was all part of the job, though there were occasions when we wished we were anywhere but sharing a night out with the Porters – those occasions when, with Leslie in high spirits, Shirley would round on him and in a voice as *sotto voce* as a buzz-saw threaten: 'Leslie, if you don't behave yourself, I'll take you home'. At times, in fact, it seemed as if he was bewitched by fear, for there was nothing he liked better than a Scotch, or three.

A sociable guy, Leslie worked as hard as he played though just occasionally the one got confused with the other, as on the memorable night when a team of us were invited for a presentation to be followed by dinner at the headquarters of International Distillers and Vintners, in Harlow. As hospitable as their name implied, there was Dom Pérignon champagne on offer when we arrived, but Leslie preferred his favourite tipple: Scotch. It came in a large tumbler, a good three-finger measure, and I don't think he realized that he was drinking his J&B Rare neat – or that his second and third tumblerfuls came neat as well. The introductions over, we proceeded to the presentation, where Leslie was shown into a front seat.

I was just behind him, and as the presentation progressed I saw him rest his head on his hand, and his elbow on the desk in front of him, and then slowly, very slowly, begin to doze off. The room was warm, the talk interminable, and little by little Leslie's elbow slipped towards the edge of the desk, until it slipped off altogether just as someone was talking-up the future prospects for the sale of Smirnoff vodka, at which point Leslie woke with a start and exclaimed, somewhat thickly: 'S'right you know, Smirnoff vodka . . .'

Then we went into dinner. A slap-up affair, all cut-glass and vintage wines, and we had reached the end of the first course when Leslie hammered on the table, rose to his feet and announced: 'Going to tell you a story of Moe the Grass, the famous Jewish informer', at which everyone fell silent and waited . . . and waited . . . and waited until Leslie apologized: 'Sorry, 's gone,' and collapsed back into his seat. The main course was as sumptuous as the entrée, and as it was being cleared away, Leslie hammered on the table for a second time, and for a second time climbed to his feet: 'Got it now. Going to tell you this story of Moe the Grass, the famous Jewish informer', and again we waited, and waited until for a second time he apologized: 'Sorry, 's gone again', and collapsed back into his seat.

Apparently, we were never to hear the story of Moe the Grass, but Leslie was undaunted, and with the liqueurs and coffee, he hammered on the table for a third time, staggered to his feet, and for a third time announced: 'Like I said, going to tell you this story of Moe the Grass, the famous Jewish informer', and then fell silent again, a silence that seemed to reach out interminably until Dennis Tuffin, one of our Directors, said very quietly: 'OK, Leslie, you just stand there and move your lips, and I'll tell the story for you'. And that's precisely what he did, which is how the main Board of IDV were entertained with the story of Moe the Grass, the famous Jewish informer.

Not that Shirley would have seen the joke. A regular martinet, she treated Leslie like a whipping-boy, and I still have a vivid memory of an apparently small incident that provided a clue to all the rest. Leslie and I had been over to the American west coast, and he had planned to meet up with Shirley in Miami on his return trip. On the day of our departure from San Francisco, Leslie came into my hotel bedroom carrying two supermarket bags crammed, hugger mugger, with clothes. To say the least, he looked distinctly unhappy, and the cause was not hard to find: 'Ian,' he said, 'd'you think I could have your suitcase to pack my things in, because if Shirley sees me carrying these,' and he held up the bags like sacrificial offerings, 'she'll kill me'. Which is how we came to swap our luggage, and Leslie lived to suffer another day!

It was a situation that I had no intention of tolerating when I succeeded Leslie as Tesco's Chairman, though I had no idea of how carefully Shirley had planned her campaign to obtain a seat on the Board until she attended the company's AGM in 1985. Everything had been going smoothly, and the transfer of power had been agreed, when a lady rose to propose Shirley as a non-executive director. Quick as a flash, she obtained a seconder, to the consternation of the Board. Clearly the whole thing had been carefully orchestrated, though whether Leslie knew of the gambit I couldn't say. For myself, I only felt embarrassment for the situation in which he found himself, though that quickly gave way to my own irritation when he turned to me and said: 'As I'm stepping down, I think it would be appropriate for our new Chairman, Ian *MacLaren*, to answer that one.'

Why the devil he should have called me 'MacLaren', I can't say. Whatever annoyance I may have felt, however, was quickly forgotten. Exactly how could I foil the proposal? Precisely what could be done to ensure that Shirley's ploy failed? The answer was an instant in coming, an instant that seemed like a lifetime, until Mike Boxall, our Company Secretary, leaned across and whispered to me: 'They're out of order. They can't elect anyone today. They have to give the meeting twenty-eight days' notice of such a proposal'. I repeated the formula, parrot-fashion: 'You have to give the meeting twenty-eight days' notice of such a proposal' and that, I thought, was that.

But there I was wrong. Shirley had other ideas. On the following Sunday, I was down in Arundel watching some cricket, when a friend came up and said: 'Have you seen the headlines in today's *Observer*?' and there it was, the lead story in the financial section: 'Tesco shareholders say "We want Shirley"'. It was the second shot in a campaign that she was to wage with unremitting ferocity for the next couple of years, punctuated by the occasional remission, as when she flirted with the idea of becoming a Euro MP, and offered herself up as a Conservative candidate for one of the outer London seats.

Such relief was generally short-lived, however; then the Old Adam would re-assert itself, and I really believe that if I had said to her: 'Give me £5 million and I'll get you on to the Board', she would have happily paid up. As it was, neither I nor the Board wanted anything of her. She was too divisive, pushy, egotistical for our liking, but the more dogged our opposition to her approaches, the more persistent she became which, I suppose, was the only thing that we had in common: our mutual determination not to concede.

The situation was an impossible one, and it finally came to a head when she rang my secretary, Jacqui, one Friday afternoon to find out what I was doing over the weekend. A woman in a hurry, it seemed that she had urgent business to discuss. Apparently, she was flying out to Israel the following week, and when Jacqui said that I was going to the FA Cup Final on Saturday afternoon, she was quick to retort: 'Oh, well, if he's going to Wembley, he can drop in and see me on his way home'. That was Shirley's way. The world revolved around her beck and call, and I was having nothing of it. If it was business she wished to discuss, then she could discuss it in office hours, and I told Jacqui to say that I would be happy to see her at any time at Tesco House.

I can see her now, electrified with anger as she paced my second floor office. When she arrived, I was busy in a meeting, and I'd arranged for Jacqui to show her into my office, to offer her coffee, and explain that I'd be with her very shortly. To wait on someone else's convenience was something that Shirley was not used to, though she was never one to neglect an opportunity to learn something to her own advantage, and when Jacqui took in her coffee, she found Shirley at my desk, rummaging through my papers. A tough lady, Jacqui had little time for Shirley's high-and-mighty ways, and was quick to point out that I did not take kindly to anyone going through my papers, and that Shirley would be well advised to sit anywhere except behind my desk.

The reprimand fused Shirley's anger. To be kept waiting was one thing. To be rebuked by a mere 'secretary' (and she made it sound as if the word should wash its mouth out) was quite another, and when I arrived a few minutes later she was incandescent with rage:

'Sorry to have kept you waiting, Shirley.' Silence.

'Would you care for another coffee?' Still nothing.

'Well, at least take a seat.'

It's an innocuous enough invitation – 'Take a seat' – but it seemed to trigger all of Shirley's pent-up fury.

'No. What I've got to say to you, I prefer to say standing up,' and then she launched into this extraordinary tirade against me: I had treated her contemptibly. I thought Leslie was a fool. I had no respect for her father's memory. And the more she raged, the more venomous she became – I was anti-Cohen, anti-semitic, anti just about everything – all punctuated by her qualifications for a place on the Tesco Board. Wasn't she Jack's daughter? Wasn't she Leslie's wife? Wasn't she the chairman of this, and a patron of that, and wasn't that enough for me?

A virtuoso performance, it was all crash, bang, wallop stuff until she had nothing left to say, and all that remained was the hatred. The thing was almost tangible, and as she stood there, marooned in the silence, I knew exactly why there could be no place for her in Tesco's future, and I told her as much: 'Look, Shirley, you'll just have to accept that as long as I am Chairman of Tesco, you'll never get a place on the Board, which is the end of the matter as far as I'm concerned.' And it was.

When I come to think about it, my only regret is that I may share some responsibility for what happened later at Westminster City Council, though there is some consolation in the fact that if she hadn't ruined the City's reputation, she could have ruined Tesco instead.

Not that she would ever admit as much, for Shirley was never a woman to say 'Sorry' or 'Thank you' for that matter. In my book they are three of the most important words in the lexicon of management. While it costs nothing to say them, however, Shirley was always too full of herself to use them. Not that she was unique. In my time, I've seen enough of the sort of self-inflating egos that flourish at other people's expense to know how damaging the habit can be. And not just to the recipients. When Blackburn Rovers began to believe that they were the greatest, when IBM began to believe in its own legend, that's when their troubles began, for as sure as pride has its fall, arrogance always gets its come-uppance – which, as I've said, is why I sometimes feel sorry for Shirley Porter, or rather, for Leslie, her husband.

There was no danger of Tesco being complacent when I took over as Chairman, however. True, we had achieved our first objective of re-positioning the company in the post-Checkout period, and true, we were already pressing Sainsbury's hard as Britain's leading retailer (there was only a 0.3 per cent gap between our market share), but those were not grounds for complacency. Quite the reverse. While the City might talk of Tesco's 'glittering performance' (the *Investors' Chronicle*), David Malpas, Mike Darnell and the rest of us knew full well that unless we set new goals for the company it would be all too easy to fall victim to our own success. Which, once again, meant appraising where we were at, and where we would like to be, not least, in our dealings with suppliers.

Traditionally, manufacturers such as Unilever and Proctor and Gamble had always been at loggerheads with multiples such as Tesco. Over terms, over contracts, over everything, the name of the game was confrontation, each party to the deal trying to screw the other down to the floor. It was an absurd situation, and one of my first actions on becoming Chairman was to talk the whole thing through with Jim Pennell, our Commercial Director, who was quick to see my point: 'What you're saying is, let's cut out the aggro, and try co-operation instead.'

And thanks to Jim and his team, our initiative worked admirably, though it took time for our suppliers to accept that we were in earnest when we said we preferred 'Jaw, Jaw' to 'War, War'. What helped, of course, was our decision that entertainment would no longer be a one-way trade. During Jack's time, there were a lot of perks about the place – a night at the opera, a freebie to God-knows-where – all provided by our suppliers. From 1986 onwards, we agreed that if we were to be entertained by our suppliers, we should entertain them in return, that we should have tickets for the opera, a box at Tottenham Hotspur, and at Lord's.

In short, what we were about was trading on equal terms, in which there would be no favours asked, and none given, and dialogue would substitute for confrontation. At first the competition were extremely hostile to our initiative, not least Sainsbury's, who continued to play their old high 'n' mighty game with their suppliers. As for the suppliers, however, their initial suspicions of our intentions were soon replaced by the recognition of the advantages to be gained from talking to us on a regular basis, to the point where, today, they are happy to sit down with the company before the launch of a new product and say: 'This is what we are hoping to do. How best can we fit in with Tesco?'

Looking back on my twelve years as Chairman, I think that this was one of my proudest achievements. For too long Tesco had traded with the notion that the only way to deal with their suppliers was by browbeating them, and believe me, our suppliers gave as good as they got in return. Twelve years on we know better, and where Tesco has led, others have followed, albeit belatedly. A quiet revolution? Possibly, but one that has transformed the entire industry over the past decade – a decade during which Tesco continued to transform itself.

Historically, the company had concentrated its operations in southern England, the Midlands, Wales, and the North West, and had found it exceptionally difficult to obtain planning consents in Yorkshire and the North East, where Asda was powerfully entrenched. In strategic terms, it was a serious deficiency which was why, in the spring of 1987, Tesco re-entered the takeover business, to reveal just how far the company had travelled in the twenty years since Jack Cohen had masterminded the takeover of Irwins and Victor Value. It was the American guru, Daniel Bell, who reflected that: 'The improvement of intuition is a highly technical matter', which is something that Jack never understood. Contemptuous as much of experts as of their expertise, he had conducted his takeover forays with all the swash-and-buckle of the retail buccaneer that he was. No question, he was successful, but by 1987 intuition had passed its sell-by date, and expertise was at a premium.

And it was this new-found expertise that we were to deploy in our bid for Hillards, a Yorkshire-based company with a first-class trading reputation. Not that we were beguiled by appearances. For six months before we made our bid, a small, multi-disciplinary team analysed every aspect of Hillards' performance. At first, they had serious reservations about the company's potential, but the more they looked into the figures, the more positive they became. In locational terms, Hillards was ideally positioned to extend Tesco's trading area into Yorkshire and the East Midlands. In image terms, the two companies complemented each other well, while the forecast was that if our bid was successful, we could triple Hillards' profits within three years.

It was only when we'd completed our research, however, that we began to finalize our bid plans. From the outset, our bankers, and Paul Smallwood of our brokers, Philips and Drew, had warned us that it would be a hard-fought battle, though I don't think we realized how tough it was going to be. Peter Hartley was running Hillards, which had been in his family for more than 100 years, and he had all the grit of a true Yorkshireman when it came to a fight. And with the family holding a 30 per cent stake in Hillards, he was in a powerful position to deal, more especially when, at the time, Tesco didn't hold a single share in the business.

A shrewd operator, Peter was quick to recognize the weakness of our position, and when I rang him to ask whether he would prefer to come to some amicable arrangement, rather than contest our bid, he was adamant. He was altogether too busy to see me – 'Going down a coal mine tomorrow' – in any case, Hillards wanted no part of a deal, and would fight Tesco to the last drop of their shareholders' blood.

Which they did. From the outset, our goal was clear: to obtain a controlling, 51 per cent stake in Hillards; and our strategy straightforward: to keep raising the stakes to what we regarded as a reasonable level, whilst mounting a blitz against existing Hillard shareholders highlighting the vulnerability of their holdings ('The competition will not allow Hillards time to re-position itself in the market . . . We do not believe that Hillards will be able to compete effectively on its own'), against the innate strengths of Tesco ('Tesco has one of the strongest retail brands in the country . . . This will secure the future of Hillards' business').

It was nerve-racking stuff, though not without its lighter moments, as when our team briefed a group of analysts from one of Hillards' major, institutional shareholders on what we intended to do with the company if our bid was successful. Lunch was over, and our audience looked distinctly somnolent even before our presentation began. And the longer it continued, the more somnolent they became, to the point where a number of them had fallen asleep. It wasn't so much that our pitch was boring, more, apparently, that they had had a very good lunch. In fact, it was only the arrival of the tea trolley that finally woke them up, to hear John Gildersleeve declaring thunderously: 'I'm sad to say that Hillards has no future unless . . .' Drowsy as they were, he left them to draw their own conclusions over their afternoon cuppa.

Those sixty days seemed interminable, but as we counted down to the statutory deadline set for such bids, it became increasingly clear that our message was getting home – even among the more sceptical City analysts. Slowly at first, but at an accelerating pace, we were winning a growing stake in Hillards – first 20, then 30, then 40 per cent of the business, until in the second week of May 1987, with our offer standing at 342.6p in cash for each of Hillards' Ordinary shares, we held 54 per cent of the company's stock.

As Peter Hartley had promised, it had been a long and bruising campaign, but the returns for Tesco were substantial, the acquisition of Hillards doing something to account for a 19 per cent increase in the company's half-year figures in 1989, and the subsequent media plaudits: 'Tesco passes the retail test with flying colours' (*The Times*) and 'Tesco is a hard rival to counter' (the

Independent). It was Roger Crowe of the *Guardian* who captured the essence of the difference the years had made since Jack's departure, however:

> A decade ago, Tesco was the modern equivalent of a music hall joke. But now it is Tesco which is laughing – all the way to the bank. It was only in the late Seventies that Tesco began discarding the 'stack it high, sell it cheap' philosophy on which the chain had been built. Then Tesco discovered what much of British industry had been learning; that people are often prepared to pay for better quality; are often concerned more with service than with price and there's often more profit in worrying about quality and service than in bribing customers with low prices. The transformation of Tesco is a remarkable success story.

The tribute was hard earned, but as far as our locational strategy was concerned, we still had some way to go. With the acquisition of Hillards we had established a powerful bridgehead in the North, but we were still under-represented in Scotland. And it was to be another five years before we were to close the gap with the purchase of Wm Low. I suspect that Jack would have been entertained by the irony. Thirty years before, he had tried to buy up the company, but had been given short shrift for his chutzpah. By 1994, however, Wm Low was beginning to struggle a bit, so I rang up Jim Miller and asked about the possibility of acquiring the business.

Concentrated as its operations were, in Scotland and the North East, Wm Low's locational profile fitted in, precisely, with Tesco's own strategic development plan, and I was delighted when Jim said, 'Let's talk'. Provided the price was right, it appeared that he was keen to deal, and after the usual haggling, we came in with a mutually agreed price of 225p for each of Wm Low's Ordinary shares. And that, we thought, was that, a constructive agreement, amicably arrived at – and then Sainsbury's trumped our bid, and came in with an offer of 300p per share.

This was just the sort of wrangle that Jack would have loved, and I remember that Board meeting vividly. Only twenty-four hours had passed since we thought we had the whole thing sewn up – which only goes to show how easy it is to fool oneself. Now, however, we had to begin again, and there were nine of us around the table when it came to deciding not so much as to whether we should take on Sainsbury's, but rather, at what price? What was the company actually worth to us, and what could we afford? If we raised our bid to 325p, then Sainsbury's could well come in at 350p, which would have ruled us out, for we all agreed that much as we valued Low, 400p per Ordinary share was too high a price to pay for the business.

It was David Reid, our Finance Director, who came up with the solution. Why not enter a forcing bid of 350p a share, and leave Sainsbury's with the dilemma of bidding up the price above Wm Low's market worth, or quitting the field? The ploy was elegant in its simplicity, though I had one reservation: 'Look, let's not go for 350, that's not the right price, let's try 360 instead'. The rest of the Board agreed: 'OK, as Chairman, you can have your extra 10p', and that's what we bid and it worked. Within two hours of our bid going in, Sainsbury's had pulled out.

I felt a little sorry for Jim Miller. He had spent a lifetime in the business, now it was over. Nonetheless he behaved impeccably throughout the negotiations, and the same went for Garry Weston when we struck a £630 million deal to buy out his two companies in Ireland – Stewarts in the North, and Quinsworth in the South. The timing of our approach couldn't have been better. As the boss of Associated British Foods, one of Tesco's major suppliers, I'd known Garry for umpteen years, but I had no idea that he was as concerned to rationalize his business by hiving off its retail element as we were concerned to obtain effective representation in Ireland. As it was, he was only too happy to trade, and in May 1997, Tesco took over Stewarts and Quinsworth in what proved to be my last major deal for Tesco.

In the late 1980s, Tesco published a selection of its Occasional Papers, *The Quiet Revolution*. By the mid-1990s the revolution was over. Both in terms of the public's perception of Tesco, and in locational terms, we had succeeded in re-positioning the company. Not that these were grounds for complacency. If we were to maintain the momentum we had achieved, then innovation remained the key to our game plan. Indeed, if there was one thing which my Tesco experience taught me, it was the fallacy of thinking that having reached the top, there was nothing more to be done. The condition, however, is commonplace, and does much to account for the failure of British industry over the past century: the mistaken belief that having become 'the workshop of the world', the rest of the world would accept our hegemony.

Once our machine tool industry had few rivals. Where is it now? Once Britain had thriving electronic and white goods sectors. Where are Pye and Ferguson and the other old names now? Once our car manufacturers – great marques such as Alvis and Riley, Rover and Rolls – could compete with the best. Now they are either defunct or sold abroad. Once, and not so distantly, we could at least trade on even terms with the rest of the world. What went wrong?

The answers are manifold – an innate suspicion of innovation; a chronic lack of sufficient investment (for long periods, the City invested £2 abroad, for every £1 at home); a congenital inability to market our products – though I suspect that one over-rides all the rest: what could well be termed the post-Imperial mindset of senior management. You can see evidence of the condition every-where – in our approach to everything from the Lords to Lord's! – and the trouble starts at the top. It is all very well managements blaming their workforce for not producing the goods, but that's a lame excuse. A workforce is only as good as its management, and all too often management in this country has been damned by its own conceit, in the City, in industry, in commerce, in sport.

Certainly, things have improved considerably in recent years, but the residue of what a former Chairman of Courtaulds called the 'Gentlemen's Club atmosphere' of management remains. The culture is as deep-rooted as it's corrosive, and I've always found it a little ironic that so many executives still appear to subscribe to the view that 'economic progress is healthy only up to a point . . . that the pursuit of efficiency of production is good only up to a point'.

In maintaining that 'small is beautiful', E. F. Schumacher tapped a powerful vein in the British psyche. Nonetheless, he was wrong. Like it or not, it is impossible to call a halt to economic progress. Either we compete effectively in what is now a global market, or we become a puppet economy. The alternative, of beating a retreat into the past – a never never land which, in prac-tice, never existed – is as damaging as it is delusive. I know. I have been there during the crisis years at Tesco when, for all his chutz-pah, Jack Cohen made an icon of the past.

Not that this is to belittle experience. Clearly, it can be invalu-able, provided, and the proviso's critical, that the past is never given free rein: 'In my forty years with the company . . . As I've always said . . . In my time as Chairman', and from their places on the walls of numberless boardrooms, an assortment of worthies-in-oil nod their approval, and silently chorus: 'Hear, hear'. A caricature, possibly, though in certain cases one that is not so remote from the truth, the more so when a company's directors all share much the same, common background, all wear much the same old school tie. And where such a situation does exist, there is always the added danger that when it comes to deciding on the line of succession, a Board will tend to perpetuate itself and, in the process, clone its own mistakes.

As far as I am concerned, diversity is the essence of a robust Board, a mix 'n' match of talents, all drawn from different walks of life, and each bringing their own expertise to the issues under discussion. At least, that is how it was during my time at Tesco. I didn't want Yes men and women around me, and I never had them. Tough, articulate, informed, the Board wanted nothing of the past, their sole concern being with the future. A headstrong experience, it was the vitality which our meetings generated that laid the foundations for the transformation of Tesco. Often as not we agreed to differ as to the means to achieve our end – and I can still hear Detta O'Cathain, one of Tesco's outstanding non-executive directors, protesting: 'But that's impossible', and David Malpas retorting: 'That's not a word in my book' – but when it came to the crunch it was always the end that counted.

Indeed, during my twelve years as Chairman, there wasn't a single occasion on which a decision was put to the vote, and I firmly believe that it was the trickle-down effect of this unanimity of purpose that helped energize the entire company. We knew where we were going though, paradoxically, we knew that we would never get there. How could we? Success is like one of those fairground cockshies, a constantly moving target. Having potted one objective, there is always the next one, and the one after that. In fact, the very idea of having achieved one's goal is a contradiction in terms, which was one reason why, two years before I retired from Tesco, we began the search for my successor.

I've always believed that there should be a cut-off point to one's stint at the top of a business. There are times in the life-cycle of a company when, like change itself, it is time for managements to recognize the need for a change. Indeed, there is a certain irony in the fact that when one does reach the top of a company, that's when they should begin to ask: How long can I maintain my momentum? When will I, too, become passé? Uncomfortable questions, maybe, but there is no escaping the reality that top managements, too, have their sell-by date. And what is true in general is doubly true during periods of unprecedented change when innovation is at a premium, and a company's success depends as much on investing in new ideas as in the Young Turks of management who have the skill and dynamic to promote them.

Of course, there is always the temptation to hang on for one grandstand finale at the AGM, one final, triumphant curtain call, which is how it was with Jack Cohen. He came to believe in his own infallibility, and in the process came close to destroying the company he had created. Albeit unwittingly, it was the final lesson that The Governor taught me – never to hang on for too long. So it was that, late in 1994, my Deputy Chairman, Victor Benjamin, David Malpas and I sat down to plan the Tesco line of succession. An outstanding lawyer, who had been on the Board for more than ten years, Victor had been the ideal sounding board for everything we had done during my Chairmanship, whilst as for David . . . thirty years had passed since he had come close to running me down in a Leicester car park, thirty years during which he had been my alter ego as much as my second-in-command. And now, for a final time, he was to place the company's best interests above his own. Although he was only a couple of years younger than me, my preference was that he should succeed me as Chairman. Indeed, my idea was that if I retired early, he would have a five-year-term in the Chair, but David was implacable. However we juggled the figures, his age was against him, and finally we came to a decision to look for a part-time Chairman, and appoint a younger man as Chief Executive, someone who would bring a fresh mind to the problems likely to face the company in the twenty-first century.

David's unselfish and down-to-earth approach was typical of the man, and in the spring of 1997, I was the last but one to hold office of the original team that had transformed Tesco. David Malpas, Dennis Tuffin, Francis Krejsa and Mike Darnell had all gone, and during my last months with the company it seemed, at times, as if the old place was haunted by memories of all that had happened since that long ago day when Jack Cohen had first said: 'If you join us, I'll give you a thousand a year and a car.' And then, Terry Leahy, our choice as the company's new Chief Executive, would burst in on my reveries: 'Ian, how about this? What d'you think of that? Thought we'd try the other.' The future was out there, waiting, again.

CHAPTER FIVE

Towards Two Thousand and One

> As advanced systems become more refined, and the wired-
> household more commonplace, there is bound to be an expan-
> sion of home delivery services to a time in the none-too-distant
> future when an as yet unquantifiable proportion of con-
> venience shopping will be handled via interactive systems.

WE STILL MEET up once a year, the Old Guard from Tesco. The
menu is as traditional (tomato soup, steak and kidney pie, followed by Christmas pudding) as the talk is nostalgic ('D'you
remember the time . . . Never forget how . . . Always laugh when I
think of . . .'), for we are more than happy to leave Terry Leahy and
his team at Tesco House to manage the future. No question, we
lived through a period of unprecedented change, though I suspect
that it was only a prelude to those still to come.

It's a fool's game trying to read the future, the more so when
I'm constantly being reminded that: 'The world is moving so fast
these days that the man who says it can't be done is generally inter-
rupted by someone already doing it'. Once something catches
your eye, it's funny how there is no escaping it, and that's the way
it is with the legend on the wall of an office around the corner
from where I now work. The concept's terrifying in its implications, the more so when contrasted with its surroundings, for at
times it seems that time itself is at a standstill within the shadow

of Big Ben. Indeed, when I first took my seat in the House of Lords, to be asked my name by a certain venerable Peer, I wondered, for a moment, whether he remembered his own. Then reality intervened, the recognition that for all the Upper House's thousand year history, discussions were already in hand to reform its entire composition.

What my ageing colleague thinks of the idea is best left to the imagination. For myself, the move is symptomatic as much of the inevitability as of the exponential rate of change: in science, in politics, in business, in our whole way of life. Which is all very well as far as it goes, the danger being that unless we carve-out the time to weigh up the consequences of change, we will become the victims rather than the beneficiaries of what Kenneth Galbraith has called 'the uncertain future'. Indeed, thinking-time is now at a premium, and if reading the future is a mug's game, it is a game that, nonetheless, has to be played.

The trouble is where to begin? Patently, there are no hard-and-fast rules when it comes to playing the future. All that's certain is that nothing's for sure. There are too many wild cards in play for that. When I was young, a sheep was a sheep. Now we have Dolly the clone. Fifty years ago, chips came wrapped in yesterday's news. Now we have chips with everything. Did I say there were no rules when it came to playing the future? I was wrong. There's one that over-rides all else – *never to say never* – for as sure as God made little apples, the unimaginable will always occur.

And what is true in general is true in particular of that most inexact of all sciences: economics. Apparently, the world is in hock to its gurus, each putting their own particular spin on the prospects for tomorrow's world. Like shamans, they read the runes, and appear on the *World at One* to permutate their options – 'It all depends what you mean by . . .' – cocksure, as ever, of their own infallibility. Yet, they remain indispensable, not least as far as retailing is concerned. Responsible, as it is, for generating almost a third of Britain's GNP, and employing, as it does, almost a fifth of the country's workforce, the industry is constantly engaged in trying to best-guess the prospects for continuing economic stability, or the likelihood of zero, or even negative growth.

In short, strategic planning is now the name of the game, a game that Tesco had to learn the hard way, but has played with increasing sophistication over the past twenty years. In fact, when I was going through my papers recently, I came across a slightly battered copy of a speech I delivered when we were still trying to take the tiger by the tail: 'Ultimately, the health, or otherwise of the retail sector, depends on the health or otherwise of the economy. Self-evident? Certainly, but one that means that we are not in the business of dealing with absolutes, rather with alternative futures.'

What applied then, applies even more so today. Talk of the globalization of the world economy has been current for a hundred years. It is only in the past quarter century, however, that the prospect has begun to be realized, with all the imponderables that that entails. A single day's headlines give some idea of the complexity of the mix: 'Japan braced for economic downturn', 'Brazilian budget deficit soars', 'Soros bets against the pound', 'Euro crisis rocks markets'.

Once all the talk was of the First World and the Third World. Notionally, at least, there is now only One World, though the notion's a myth as I learned for myself on a visit to India as Chairman of the England and Wales Cricket Board. The conference over, Ann and I went on a seven-day tour of Rajasthan. It was a wonderful yet horrific experience: wonderful to see some of the great monuments of India's past; horrific to see them surrounded by such poverty and squalor. There we were, travelling first class, and there, just beyond the windows of our air-conditioned coach, was another world, a nightmare world of hungry faces and upturned hands begging for a pittance. For all the fine talk of One World, the Two Worlds still remain.

Quite coincidentally, on my return I had a call from a specialist in international affairs, Raffie Kaplinsky, of the Institute of Development Studies, asking whether I would consider supporting a project to examine the problems implicit in the polarization of the world economy. I was only too happy to help him as far as I could. If we are to create an equitable global economy, then it's critical that the problem is addressed with the urgency that the situation demands. The alternative is too fearsome to contemplate: of growing divisions leading to confrontations.

Located at the interface between supply and demand, 'The Shop' has always been one of the most sensitive indicators of shifts in the economy, and as such, the retailer has always been in the business of trying to gauge the mood of the market. When relatively little capital was required to establish and run a business, it was a comparatively primitive occupation. No longer. Today, when multiples such as Tesco, Sainsbury's and M&S are committed to multi-million-pound development budgets, a sophisticated appraisal of the likely impact of mid- and long-term socio-economic conditions is critical to their success.

How will the economy perform, either inside or outside the Euro? What impact will demographic changes (not least, of an ageing population) have on consumer expenditure? What legislative measures (on food policy, car usage, work practices) will condition the industry's marketing and development strategies? How will climatic change/global warming affect the retail business? How will people spend their disposable income, and how much will they have to spend? The questions multiply, and with them the multiplicity of the answers for, once again, there can be no absolutes when it comes to playing the future. Yet the attempt has to be made.

I won't go as far as to say that I have seen the future and it works, I'm not that much of an optimist, but I am reasonably confident that the UK economy will remain relatively stable into the mid-term. Clearly, there will be the occasional hiccup (the occasional tendency for the economy to over-heat, and the consequent deflationary pressures) but overall, the prospects look good for a period of steady-state growth. Of course, there are always the doomwatchers who say that whatever the state of the economy, there must be a limit to growth, that at sometime in the future, consumer demand will be satiated. If history is anything to go by, their argument certainly does not stand up.

* * *

Some time ago, I was reading a piece about the 1930s Mercedes Benz – a monstrous creation generating 228 horse power – that came close to winning at Le Mans. With a top speed of more than 120mph, it was widely regarded as the ultimate machine. And now? Now, as a result of continual improvement in motor vehicle design and performance, what was once regarded as a miracle of engineering is a commonplace specification of many family saloons. And as with engineering, so with every other aspect of the economy. An ever-receding target, the market never reaches saturation point, for change is innate – the more so when the economy is in a state of rapid transition and the meaning of work is being redefined.

The development has been a progressive one, and like so much else it is progressively gaining in momentum. Indeed, it tends to be forgotten that, as late as 1960, manufacturing, and more especially Britain's 'smokestack industries', employed almost eleven million people – more than double the number in the service industries. Forty years on, the situation has been reversed, the service sector workforce having trebled, and the manufacturing workforce having been halved. The speed and extent of this transformation is unprecedented, and the adaptation time has been foreshortened. It took a century and more to come to terms with the impact of the Industrial Revolution. We have much less time to come to terms with its post-industrial variant, not least if the latest forecast that by 2020 the working week will have shrunk to twenty-five hours because of 'technology inspired productivity gains' is realized.

The phrase captures the essence of the transformation taking place in our working lives. In fact, 'traditional' jobs are fast becoming the stuff of legend. In the last five years alone, two-thirds of the jobs that have been created have not been on a permanent basis, and the probability is that in the very near future the continuing decline of jobs in the manufacturing sector will be paralleled by an increase in short-term, fixed-term or part-time work; in a rise in the number of people holding two, or even three jobs; in the growth of the number of computer-based home-workers; and by a continuing gender shift in the composition of the workforce.

It's half a lifetime ago since Jack Cohen rejected my plea to pay Daisy Hyams a wage comparable with Tesco's other directors with the blunt assertion: 'Oh, she's married. She doesn't need the money'. He was not alone with his prejudice. Sexism was then deep-rooted in the culture of management, a macho belief that women were second-rate citizens, incapable of holding down responsible jobs. An absurd notion, which not only denied women the opportunities their talents deserved, but also deprived the economy of those skills being put to good use. Thirty years on, the situation is slowly being redressed, and not before time.

There is a continual need to re-think what we are about, not least as far as the future of work is concerned. For instance, it seems to me that there is an increasingly tenuous balance between the growing number of women in employment, and the potential of advanced systems to destroy jobs. Only recently, I was talking to the assistant manager of a bank in Hertfordshire, and his story was too commonplace for comfort: 'I joined the bank when I was seventeen thinking that I'd got a job for life. Now I come in every morning and wonder whether my job's still there, or whether I've been replaced by some new system, and if so, what will I do with the rest of my life?'

It's a big question. At forty-six years of age, what *will* he do with the thirty or so years that remain to him? Not that he's alone. Far from it. There are lots of people like him around, people who opted for the sort of job security that no longer exists. And it is not just advanced systems that are causing the problem. A company is taken over, and there's the redundancy package on the table, and the next thing an individual knows is that he's run out of time. He may have been with the same company for years, then suddenly he has no place to go. There are a huge number of stories like that out there, and we are going to hear more and more of them, more especially as we have to come to terms with an ageing population.

Of course, there can be no question about the benefits to be achieved from company rationalization, or the capacity of advanced systems to improve productive efficiency. As always, however, the benefits to be gained have to be carefully weighed against their possible drawbacks. Once the equation was that if two-thirds of the population were 'economically active', it meant that they could support the other one-third – the kids at school, the old, the handicapped, and those who, for one reason or another, were unable to work.

But what if the situation is reversed? What, if as a result of technological developments, only one-third of the population is economically active, and two-thirds are dependent on the income they generate? What then? How will it be possible to provide the pensions, the schools, and the hospitals, that are the staples of our way of life? And this is by no means all. What if a time should come when even those people who do hold down jobs have time to spare on their hands? It was the American futurologist, Hermann Kahn, who predicted that in the none-too-distant future, the traditional formula of the Three 48s – a 48 hour working week, a 48 week working year, and a 48 year working life – would be replaced by the Three 35s – a 35 hour working week, a 35 week working year, and a 35 year working life.

Since he wrote, working hours have risen rather than fallen, but what if Kahn is eventually proved to have been right? What of a time when the majority of the population spends only a small proportion of its time at work? Precisely how will people adapt to working at leisure? True, it is only a forecast, but if realized it will revolutionize Britain's lifestyle.

Not that this revolution will be uniform. Inevitably it will be conditioned by differences in the spending power of individual households, leisure meaning something quite different to the £60,000 a year executive than to the jobless, or the worker on a third of that income. Henry Ford was one of the first people to realize that unless he paid his workforce a decent wage, they would never be able to afford his Model T. In short, if wages are seriously depressed, it inevitably leads to a reduction in demand, with all that entails as far as the economy is concerned.

This, of course, is to doomwatch, but if such a situation should arise, how will each group respond? How will they spend their discretionary time? The answer, I suspect, lies in the relationship between income and time: *upper income earners spending money to save time: lower income earners spending time to save money.*

Clearly there will be a huge range of variables between the

extremes, though there are already signs of this polarization in the use of our leisure time. In the past couple of decades we have seen the explosive growth of DIY. I suspect that for those people with limited incomes, DIY activities will play a significant role in tomorrow's world. And what of the rest, of those with money but limited time? Again, it is possible to read something of the future in the immediate past: in the still-to-be-realized, full potential of tele-shopping. It's now twelve years ago since I floated the idea at the International Centre for Companies of the Food Trades and Industry (CIES) Conference in Vienna:

> Could it be that as far as this income group is concerned, we are seeing the last generation of the traditional, convenience store? Could it be that in future, upper income groups will shop via TV, for their goods to be home delivered and paid for by credit transfer? A fanciful notion? Not so. By early in the twenty-first century 'tele-shopping' could well account for a fifth and more of this affluent market.

I was wrong. The prospect is that the figure will be more than doubled in the years immediately ahead, while the better-off will buy in additional services as and when required. Not that this is anything new. The reverse. Until World War I, the majority of homes provided their own goods and services, whilst servicing the more affluent, the irrepressible Mrs Beeton listed the twenty-five 'domestics' from butler and cook to gardener and scullery maid, each with their appropriate salaries (£50 annually for the butler, £5 to £9 for the scullery maid) that composed a 'gentleman's household'.

The same conditions could re-emerge in post-industrial societies, though in a totally different context. Indeed, the problems posed by changes in the social structure could well be resolved by the development that has generated them: technology. On the assumption that time is a tradeable commodity, advertisements are already appearing in the US offering to act as 'time managers' for executive households with little of the commodity to spare. Employing highly sophisticated databases, they marry a range of services, many of which are, themselves, dependent on advanced, domestic appliances, to those who require them.

It's early days, but could this become a new growth sector in the economy? Certainly being 'of service' rather than 'in service' is more in keeping with the modern age in which many people find the old, hierarchical relationships distinctly uncomfortable, preferring, instead, to employ technology-mediated services.

The imponderables multiply, and with them the questions. Clearly all the above factors will impact directly on the structure of retailing, whilst cumulatively they will re-shape its entire character. The problem, yet again, is to determine what shape this character will take, for it seems that the only certainty about the future of work is uncertainty itself.

Only one thing, in fact, is sure: that whatever form the redefinition of work and leisure take, they will demand a corresponding response from retailers. If part-time and broken-time working become the norm; if the shift in the gender structure of employment continues (it's recently been forecast that by 2020 one in five fathers will be 'house husbands', and their wives will be the breadwinners); if there is a significant reduction in working hours, with a consequent increase in people's 'disposable time', then it is almost inevitable that shopping hours will continue to extend, until round-the-clock shopping, on a round-the-week basis will be the rule rather than the exception.

Indeed, Tesco has already been experimenting with twenty-four-hour shopping at a number of pilot stores, and I still remember my astonishment on visiting a store at two in the morning and finding it crowded with customers, among them couples in evening dress who appeared to regard the experience as a natural extension of their night on the town. If not the world, then it is time that's being turned upside down. And as with twenty-four-hour shopping, so with Sunday opening. The present, six hour time limit – six hours during which Tesco takes more money per hour than at any other period during the week – is certain to go, if only as a result of public demand.

And it was public demand, that came close to overwhelming Tesco at the launch of its home delivery service. Based on research which showed that a high proportion of residents in the Twickenham area of south-west London were two-income households who would welcome the provision of such a service, the take-up rate for the experiment exceeded the company's most optimistic projections. Seemingly, history does repeat itself, the difference being that where working partnerships don't always have the time to do their own shopping, the very idea of shopping for her groceries would have been quite foreign to my mother. It just wasn't done. She would pick up the phone on Thursday morning and place her order, and on Saturday morning the delivery boy would pedal up to our gate on his bike with her order: a small symbol of status in the outer suburb of London where we lived.

While status may be important, it is now a secondary consideration to convenience, to the provision of a service which allows people to maximize the use of their disposable time. As such, home delivery services are sure to expand, the more so with the application of technology. Twenty years after Tesco pioneered computer-based, home-shopping in Gateshead. The development is still in embryonic form, but not for very much longer. As advanced systems become more refined, and the wired-household more commonplace, there is bound to be an expansion of home delivery services to a time in the none-too-distant future when an as yet unquantifiable proportion of convenience shopping will be handled via interactive systems. The implications of such a development are profound. Could it mean the end of 'The Shop' as we know it? One can never say never, though I doubt it. For many people shopping today is as much a social as an essential occupation, a leisure time pursuit to be enjoyed rather than endured.

In fact, the lay-out of modern stores has created a significant shift in the public's perception of their shopping experiences. Designed specifically to be user-friendly, large out-of-town stores are no longer the bogey that they once were. Nonetheless, there is still a significant difference between how people perceive and shop in such stores. Once Tesco believed that there was little to differentiate between convenience and comparison shopping. With the opening of our first, joint venture with M&S, we discovered how wrong we had been. Where, previously, we had believed that people would enjoy one-stop shopping, research quickly revealed that 85 per cent of our joint custom would shop first at Tesco, then go home, and return later to visit M&S.

In short, we were dealing with two, quite different mindsets: one which regarded convenience shopping as a chore; the other that regarded comparison shopping as a leisure pursuit. Although a lot has been done to close this perception 'gap' it still remains, as does the question: What of the future for 'The Shop', or more precisely, of the large, out-of-town developments? Having just reached maturity, are they already passing their sell-by date? Like the corner shops of Jack Cohen's era, are they already becoming monuments to the past? Clearly not. They are now an established part of the retail hierarchy, though it is unlikely that many more will be opened. Indeed, it may not be entirely coincidental that the government's decision to embargo the development of such units occurred at much the same time as evidence was accumulating of an acceleration in the so-called 'flight from the cities'.

There is nothing new in this of course. During 1930s, the expansion of suburban railways led to the sort of sub-urban sprawl damned by Osbert Lancaster as 'Bypass Variegated', each with its ubiquitous parade of small shops; the staple of Jack's burgeoning empire. Then he was catering for the 'nine-to-five' commuter. Now, with the growth of broken- and flexi-time working, with the increase in the number of out-workers operating from computer terminals in their homes, and with the dispersal of the support services of many major companies, the old space–time boundaries have diminishing relevance.

Since leaving Tesco, I've been fortunate to find a flat in the centre of London. Previously, it had been one small part of a large office block occupied by a major commercial concern, which opted a couple of years ago to relocate out-of-town, along the M4 corridor. In this, they are not alone. On the contrary, what might be called the technological dispersal of population, powered by interactive systems that provide instant communication regardless of the distances involved, is as much a matter of commercial judgement as it is of personal preference.

Ann and I are lucky. We have been able to keep our home in Hertfordshire, whilst having a pied-à-terre in London. Consequently, we are able to permutate our options as to where we shop, and in the process, compare what's happening in our inner-cities with what is happening out-of-town. As to the one, Tesco anticipated the growing needs of commuters, and more especially, of working women, with the opening of its first Metro store in Covent Garden in 1996. Jack Cohen would have been proud of it. Covering little more than 12,000 square feet, much the same size as one of his own, much-beloved supermarkets, and heavily dependent on advanced systems to service demand, Covent

Garden now caters for more than 80,000 customers a week, and on a square-foot basis takes more money than any other store operated by the company.

Apparently, the retail cycle is turning full circle, the more so with the recent development of Tesco Express, small units, little larger than the traditional village shop, attached to petrol filling stations, that stock a full range of household provisions. But if a new generation of stores is emerging (or should that read re-emerging?) to service the needs of inner-city residents and commuters, what of places such as Hertfordshire? The official forecast is that over the next fifteen years, more than a million new homes will be needed in south-east England alone resulting, in part, from changing social structures, in part, from the continuing flight from the cities.

If the projections are correct, it will provide retailers with both an opportunity and a challenge: the opportunity of helping to restore life to our ailing town centres; the challenge of playing a constructive role in the creation of the new satellite communities already under consideration. As to the former, the first and most urgent need is to protect our existing towns from the depredations of the car and, in consequence, improve their overall quality of life. The government is already committed to curbing indiscriminate car usage. It won't be an easy job. The car has become the icon of our times, albeit an equivocal one.

For twenty years, I would get up around six in the morning to beat the jams whenever I had to drive into London. If I left it any later, it would take me two hours or more to cover the thirty-mile journey – two hours of unrelieved misery. I'd become so conditioned to driving that I never really considered the alternative – public transport. Not that I was alone, and if I was running late I'd join the tailback with the hundreds-and-thousands – one, or at most two to a car – from the city's outskirts into the centre. I must have been crazy, for if I had only bothered to make the five minute drive to my local station, I could have halved my journey time, and travelled in much greater comfort.

The government will have a hard time reversing our love affair with the car, and however good their intentions, they will be undermined unless paralleled by what is so often lacking – the provision of effective public transport systems to service existing centres. Given an integrated transport policy, however, it could lead to the renaissance of many of Britain's town centres. Of course, the retail mix will be different, the emphasis being on comparison rather than convenience shopping. Nonetheless, the potential for such a revival is huge; in effect, of making our towns the user-friendly places they were before the coming of the car.

But this is only half of the equation. Only so much residential in-filling is possible in our existing urban centres. What of the remainder of the million new homes that will be required by 2016? Where will they go? Of course, the problem is not new. There can be no question about the idealism that motivated the New Town movement, the trouble being when it came to turning the good intentions into practice. In their early days, many of the New Towns created almost as many problems as they resolved, not least due to lack of effective service provision of pubs and cafés, shops and libraries, and all those little extras that are critical to the quality of everyday life.

Since then, the mistakes of the past have been rectified. They mustn't be allowed to happen again. If extensive developments are to transform the character of certain of our smaller towns-cum-villages, and the government has already indicated that they believe that 10,000 houses are a minimum requirement if such communities are to be self-supporting, then it is essential that planners think through the needs not only of the existing residents, but also of the off-comers. And this, as I see it, means pre-planning the development of effective facilities to service the needs of both.

* * *

A quarter of a century has passed since Tesco submitted proposals to the government for the establishment of integrated service facilities in London's Docklands. The idea was a simple but nonetheless elegant one: that rather than dispersing such facilities – a shop here, a library there, a leisure centre somewhere else – they should be concentrated at the core of the development, and well served by public transport. The object? To minimize (and this was the operative word) car usage by providing families with all those small but nonetheless important facilities they needed on one central and sensitively planned site – a place where my mother could do her shopping, or have a coffee with her friends; where my father could drop in to the library, or enjoy a quiet pint; where the kids could meet up with their pals, and play in safety. In short, we were proposing the creation of a new model 'town centre' that would replicate the best features of old, until, that is, so many of them became snarled-up with traffic.

The trouble being that while it took time for our historic town centres to develop – an organic process spanning centuries – time is no longer on the planners' side. The pressures to resolve the problem are too great for that. Given imagination, however, there is no reason why such 'new towns' should not only provide the new homes required in the years immediately ahead, but also the quality of services their new residents expect and deserve. And, as always in this context, retailers can and should play a positive and constructive role. Traditionally, at the core of community life, they can do as much to create an attractive environment for our new-towns-in-embryo, as they can to revive our existing town centres.

But then, I'm an optimist – with the caveat that there can be no absolutes when it comes to reading the future. Whichever of my various scenarios is realized, however, one factor will condition them all: advanced systems. No question about their capacity to transform the world in which we live, or don't, for that matter. At times, in fact, it's a prospect that boggles the mind, of a world of virtual reality in which nothing really exists. A nightmare? Possibly, though one that is not so far removed from the truth. It's more than twenty years now since Donald Harris, Tesco's computer boffin, told me a cautionary tale.

One morning he'd arrived at Tesco House at around 7.30 a.m., and on going up to the computer suite, found that his sub-boffins were already there, logged-on to their computers. The following day, he arrived earlier still, and they were there again. This went on until he arrived at 6.30 a.m. – and there they were, at it again. And much the same applied in reverse each evening. When everyone else had left their offices, at 5 p.m., 6 p.m., or 7 p.m., he'd call in to see what was going on on the third floor, and whatever the hour, they were still at it – little more than extensions of their machines. As far as Donald was concerned, this was carrying dedication to extremes, and it worried him enormously: 'D'you know, I've got a nasty feeling that they can only communicate with their screens'.

Now that is a nightmare, a world in which reality does, indeed, become virtual. And what applies in general, applies in particular to senior management. With all the hardware that's available today, there is always the danger of executives becoming dependent on smart systems to do their thinking for them. It is a temptation that has to be resisted. Business leaders are not automatons, programmed into their systems, and once they start believing that it is possible to beat the future by reading the runes off their screens, that's where their troubles begin.

There can be no question, of course, about the role that advanced systems now play in powering the economy, having helped to raise Britain's GDP by 40 per cent in the past two decades, though in doing so, they have contributed to the growing disparities between what are now euphemistically described as the 'work rich' and the 'work poor'. Indeed this is the central dilemma posed by the systems themselves: that no one doubts their capacity to produce 'technology inspired productive gains', rather our own capacity to ensure that such gains are distributed on a reasonably equitable basis. The alternative can only lead to socio-economic polarization, examples of which I saw during my tour of Rajasthan.

Yet this is the One World in which retailers now trade, and not only for the produce stacked on their supermarket shelves. Where Jack Cohen could see little further than the corner shop, British multiples now think in global terms as far as investment is concerned – though as Sainsbury's discovered in the States, and Tesco learned during its short-lived foray into France, it's a tough old world out there. As a first venture into the continental market, Tesco bought a controlling stake in Catteau, a mid-sized supermarketing chain centred on Lille, in the early 1990s. Maybe we were in a bullish mood because the company was doing so well, or maybe it was because we thought that we could teach the French a lesson or two. After all, wasn't it Napoleon who called us a nation of shopkeepers? Whatever the case, Tesco met its Waterloo with Catteau, and one of Terry Leahy's first moves on becoming Chief Executive was to pull out of the business, and I thoroughly applauded his decision.

The Catteau experience was a costly one, though it did teach us one lesson: that there is little to be gained from making such an investment unless it is possible to get some sort of brand leadership position – and the big French operators, who are very good indeed, made damned sure that never happened in Catteau's case. And what applied to Catteau, applies equally well for most of Western Europe and the States.

When I was Chairman of Tesco we looked very carefully at the North American market, and found that there was a significant difference in cultural attitudes to shopping over there. In the UK the development of own labels has been very strong indeed, whereas in the States, customers are very brand-orientated, and tend to regard 'own labels' as very inferior products. It's nonsense, of course, but as Sainsbury's and M&S have learned, it's a difficult job to change established mindsets, which is one reason why, after examining the situation in detail, we turned our face absolutely against going into the US.

Of equal importance was the recognition that the US, as with much of Western Europe, is extremely well shopped, in contrast to the former Eastern Bloc countries. Where they could produce the goods, they could not get them into the shops, and where they could get them into the shops, they were never in sufficient quantities, and queuing became a feature of everyday life – as I saw on a visit to the Soviet Union with a party arranged by John Gummer, the best Minister of Agriculture with whom I ever had dealings. It was a disturbing experience. There was no question about the Russians' capacity to raise crops, they had had a wonderful harvest. Lacking an effective chill chain in which to store their produce, however, they lived with a glut of foodstuffs for a couple of months, then ploughed the remainder into the ground. Perhaps it is not altogether fanciful to say that the collapse of the Soviet empire was due, in part, to its inability to deliver the goods!

Since the Berlin Wall came down all that has changed or, rather, is changing. In the past nine years, the former Warsaw Pact countries have begun to make up for the fifty lost years of Soviet rule. In 1994 Tesco bought the Global group in Hungary, and the hypermarket we opened in Budapest is the most successful single unit the company has ever opened, whilst in 1996 Tesco went into Czech and Slovakia, having acquired the K Mart business, and I'm told that the thirteen or fourteen stores that the company is now operating there are trading very successfully indeed. And that's only a beginning, for it suggests that given the right developments on the right sites, there are still huge market opportunities to be tapped in Eastern Europe.

Not that this is to forget the lesson that Tesco learned from Catteau of the importance of brand leadership – or of never underestimating the competition. The Germans, the Italians and the French are all in there slugging it out for a slice of the business, as they are, increasingly, in the global market. In fact, Carrefour is to all intents and purposes already a global operator, and where they have led, others will follow. So much is inevitable, for as with virtually every other business, the world is now the retailers' market place, and I am sure that the prospect of expanding eastwards, not least, into the Pacific rim, is now high on the agenda of every UK multiple – as confirmed by the fact that, even as I write, it has just been announced that Tesco has bought a controlling stake in the Thai market.

And if European and US multiples are set to become global players, then it is equally likely that the trend will be towards mega-mergers on a global scale, as is already happening in other sectors as exemplified by the recent Vodafone–AirTouch deal. No question, Jack Cohen would have welcomed the prospect – a reprise of his own, palmy days. While it is all very well to 'think global', however, companies do so at their peril if it is at the expense of their home base. Of course, the temptation of thinking big is always there, of spinning the globe and permutating one's fantasies. What of Taiwan? Why not Korea? How about the Philippines?

Unless a company has secured its home market, it is a dangerous game to play, while it is even more dangerous to think that it is possible to export one's problems to cover deficiencies at home. Overseas investment is all very well just as long as it does nothing to weaken a company's position in the market that is generating its prime source of income and if, for instance, Tesco were to go off the boil because of its overseas ventures, it could put the whole business at risk. Not that I'm suggesting that companies should 'think small', rather that they should think hard before committing themselves to expansion overseas. As I've said, it is a tough old market out there, and the competition give no hostages to fortune.

But then, that has always been the case in the retail business, the risks entailed being proportional to the scale of investment involved. In 1919, Jack Cohen staked his £30 war gratuity on a barrow-load of surplus stock. To him, it was the ultimate risk, a decision that was to transform the pattern of much of British retailing. Eighty years on, much the same remains true, the difference being in the size of the investment involved, and the consequent risks entailed.

Ultimately, however, it is the decision-taking capacity of managements that will determine how their companies perform in an uncertain future. And high-tech is no substitute for that capacity. Unquestionably, advanced systems can play an important role when it comes to reading the future, but when it comes to the crunch it is down to individuals, such as Terry Leahy and his team at Tesco House, who have to determine whether or not the investment's worth making, the risk's worth taking. Which is why, when we meet for our annual junket at the Old Fire Engine House restaurant in Ely, the Tesco Old Guard are quietly confident that the future of the company is safe in their hands.

Captain of the cricket team at Shrewsbury House Prep School in 1949.

The same at Malvern in 1955.

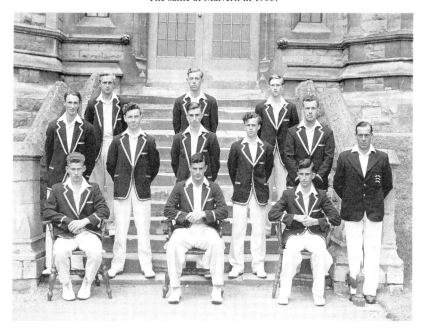

With my parents and wife Ann (standing) in 1960.

The Tesco board in 1971 with a model for a new store. (*standing from l to r*)
Robin Behar, David Behar, George Wood, Lawrence Leigh and me, (*seated from l to r*)
Alfred Singer, Hyman Kreitman, Jack Cohen, Leslie Porter and Daisy Hyams.

At the opening of Crawley Tesco in 1974 with (*from l to r*) Jack Cohen,
Albert Redford, the store manager, and George Wood.

Left: Jack Cohen presents Daisy Hyams with her OBE hidden in a golden can of baked beans.

Below: Daisy Hyams and Shirley Porter greet Princess Anne at the dinner to celebrate 50 years of Tesco PLC.

With Prime Minister Margaret Thatcher on a visit to her local Tesco in Finchley. She often used to pop in.

John and Norma Major on the campaign trail in 1997 at Cheltenham Tesco.

My family (*from l to r*): Ann, Gillian, Neil and Fiona.

My introduction to the House of Lords in November 1996 with my sponsors Lord Macfarlane and Baroness O'Cathain. *Universal Pictorial Press and Agency Ltd*

Celebrating Europe's victory in the Ryder Cup with Seve Ballesteros
and my daughter, Gillian, September 1997.

Discussing tactics with then captain Mike Atherton on the tour
of Zimbabwe in winter 1997. *Graham Morris*

With cricket youngsters at Trent Bridge in 1998, presenting a cheque for £1.5 million for Nottingham CC. *Graham Morris*

At Lord's with captain Alec Stewart, February 1999. *Allsport*

CHAPTER SIX

A View from the City

> The contrast with Tesco was extraordinary. Where we maintained a dialogue with our own people and our customers as a matter of company policy, it seemed to me that the hierarchs at the Nat West had little time for either.

MY MOTHER HAD much in common with the Old Guard at the National Westminster Bank. Both regarded trade as taboo, and as I walked into the HQ of the bank on that day in 1990 as a non-executive director, I recalled what she had said on learning that I had accepted Jack Cohen's offer of thousand a year and a car: 'I haven't spent all this money on your education for you to join a company like Tesco'. Thirty years on, the stigma remained, to be peddled *sotto voce*, as if the word itself was contagious: 'You know, that chap MacLaurin's joined us. Good fella, of course, but comes out of trade'. A caricature, perhaps, but on my first day in Lothbury, I couldn't help reflecting on the irony that the City itself had been built upon trade – and that banks are little more than retailers in money, and other people's money at that.

Indeed, even after accepting the Bank's offer, I had serious reservations about my decision. After all, I knew little about the arcane world of banking, and I already had a business to run. Victor Benjamin, Tesco's Deputy Chairman, however, thought differently, and it was to be a couple of years before I forgave him for persuading me to accept the appointment: 'Go on, Ian, give it a go. You've got a great deal to offer, and nothing to lose'. I was soon to learn otherwise, for my introduction to Lothbury set the tone of much that was to follow, until the Chairman, Lord Alexander, began to impose his authority on the Nat West regime. And in the highly conservative environment of the City, that took time. Meanwhile I ran the gauntlet of the flunkeys who patrolled the Bank's reception, and was ushered up to the inner sanctum of Nat West power.

The setting was as impressive as the mood was reverential. This was no ordinary business that we were about. This was something quite different, and as we settled into our seats, and shuffled through our papers, I wondered at the contrast with Tesco. Where our Board meetings were rumbustious, even combustible affairs, my first and abiding impression was that Nat West Boards were the products of meticulous stage-management, the Bank's executives having carefully pre-planned their strategy to ensure that even if awkward questions were asked, they would receive only the most anodyne of replies.

Or no replies at all, for they never got round to my query which, if I remember, had something to do with projected returns on the Bank's investment in the US. Time, it seemed, was pressing, luncheon being an integral part of the ritual, and at 12.50 precisely, the meeting ended and we broke up for drinks. What Victor would have made of it all, I can't say. For myself, it seemed that I'd been inducted into a magic circle totally divorced from reality, and as I returned to Tesco that afternoon I wondered not so much as what I had to offer, as what I had got to lose. The kudos that went with the appointment was all very well, but as far as I was concerned, non-executive directors should play a positive, even an abrasive role in a company's business, rather than impersonating the dormouse in *Alice in Wonderland*, curiosities to be aired at Board meetings on a once-a-month basis before being popped back into the executive teapot. God knows, I had never regarded myself as a dormouse, and I didn't intend to begin now, more especially with the experience of Enterprise Oil behind me.

Enterprise Oil was my first, non-executive venture outside Tesco, and when Peter Walker, then Secretary of State for Energy, rang to ask if I would join the Enterprise Board, he made no bones about what he was looking for: a commonsense approach to the business. When I told him that the only oil I knew anything about was olive oil, he laughed, but insisted; 'Look, we want people with practical business experience on the Board in the countdown to privatization, which is why I'm calling you'. A little flattery goes a long way, and when I raised the matter with Leslie Porter, then Chairman of Tesco, he not only agreed to the appointment, but actively encouraged me to take on the job in the belief that such directorships were very much a two-way trade: that I would both contribute to the Enterprise project, and at the same time learn from the experience. Indeed, his only caveat, and it applied to the entire Tesco Board, was we should not over-extend ourselves by taking on more than two non-executive roles. And Leslie was right.

As I see it, there are two sorts of non-executives, those who get into a business, and really learn what it's about, and those who turn up every month or six weeks, skim through their papers, then pick up their money and run. In part, of course, it is the fault of companies who flatter themselves by recruiting the great and the good, but what's the use of having my name up there on the letter-head when most of the staff say: 'MacLaurin? MacLaurin? Who the devil's he?' Not that there is any shortage of candidates who are only too happy to indulge in such misplaced vanity, characters who make a profession of collecting non-executive directorships like those 'sticky little things, stamps'.

The only way a non-executive can contribute effectively to a company's business is by getting to grips with the running of the business itself, and that means more than simply reading the papers on the monthly agenda. However good the minutes, the papers, and the background briefings are, they can never provide a real 'feel' for what a company is all about. To do that means getting out there, beyond the ghetto of the executive suite, and meeting people who are doing the job on the ground, as was the case with John Gardiner. We first met as non-executives on the Enterprise Board, and when Stuart Young, one of Tesco's directors died, I invited John to join the Tesco Board. At first, he wasn't at all keen on the idea – 'Look, Ian, I know nothing about selling baked beans, and I'm not interested in the business in any case,' – but eventually I managed to persuade him: 'All right, if you really want me I'll do three years, but no more'. That was thirteen years ago, and in the interim, during which he has become the Chairman of Tesco, I suspect that John's come to like the idea of selling baked beans.

In the early 1980s, however, we had other things on our mind, for Enterprise couldn't afford to carry any hangers-on in the run-up to flotation. In the highly volatile state of the oil market, the Chief Executive, Graham Hearne, ran a tight operation, and there were no freeloaders when it came to the monthly Board meetings. Ultimately, good management is all about team building. As a Chairman or Chief Executive you've got to get hold of people who are very different in temperament, background, and skills, but who will work well together. It's a bit like what it takes to make a good Test team, each of the eleven bringing his own skills to the game, but all being motivated by the same aim: to win. Once you get that sort of cohesion, you are well on the way to putting together a good side. That's what I tried to do at Tesco, and the results spoke for themselves.

Not that it is an easy job. Being a director of major PLC means that you carry a huge responsibility to your customers, to your shareholders, and perhaps most important of all, to your staff for, come the crunch, they are the people who make the whole operation tick. There's nothing to be gained, and all to be lost, by playing the great 'I Am', and I still remember Jack Cohen's advice to me in the early days of my career with Tesco: 'Ian, always remember that the most important person in this organization is the chap on the back door'. As ever, Jack's advice was self-interested, because it was the chap out the back who was responsible for signing in all the goods, and without them our stores would have been in trouble. In my book, however, there is more to it than self-interest, for the most important person in any organization is, indeed, the metaphorical chap on the back door, and however you may fancy yourself, you should always have time for those people in the company who open the door for you.

Everyone has a part to play in the teams that make up a business today, and when you've got your people buying into your vision, you are well on the way to where you want to go. Which was how it was with Enterprise Oil. We knew just where we were going until, that is, the oil market collapsed. In the five years to 1986, crude oil prices fell from $38 to $10 a barrel, and when Enterprise was floated it was too highly priced, and only half the offer was taken up. In the resulting hiatus, RTZ made a bid for the entire company but eventually we were able to sort the whole thing out.

Of course, Enterprise had one, important advantage: by its very nature, it had never had to cope with a family's dynastic ambitions. Jack had tried to perpetuate the Cohen line, and failed, and for a century and more Sainsbury's have succeeded in 'keeping it in the family' – and not always to their own or the company's advantage. Peter Davies became Sainsbury's Deputy

Chairman at much the same time as I was appointed Deputy Chairman of Tesco, and I'll never forget the subsequent conversation we had on the phone. I'd known Peter for years, and I can still recall his reply when I rang to congratulate him on his appointment: 'The difference between your job and mine, Ian, is that you know perfectly well that one day you'll become the Chairman of Tesco, while I know perfectly well that I'll never become the Chairman of Sainsbury's'.

The remark was revealing as much for what it said about the management of Sainsbury's as about the problems that it can cause, and I think that even David Sainsbury would agree that his time as Chairman of the company was not an altogether successful one. In fact, I suspect that if I had been in his place, and had produced the results that Sainsbury's had done, the institutions would have tackled the non-executive directors and demanded my dismissal. Which does nothing to diminish the extent of Sainsbury's achievements. On the contrary, the hiccup in the company's performance was significant only because it was so unusual. Since John Sainsbury opened his first store in Drury Lane, the company had been a dynamic element in British retailing, the benchmark by which Tesco judged its own performance.

Not that the problems of dynastic succession can be compared with the problems involved, and the risks entailed, when managements recycle themselves and, in the process, recycle their own inadequacies. There is nothing new about networking, of course. Long before the Old School Tie came into fashion, the Old Boy school of patronage had become the norm. So much, I suppose, is inevitable – a matter not so much of what you know as who you know – and while the practice can be beneficial, there is always the danger that management will become an exclusive preserve, a freemasonry committed to perpetuating its own hegemony.

Which was how it was for far too long in British business, not least in the City, effectively the preserve of a handful of powerful families. Indeed, I've always felt there was something a trifle ironic in the fact that the City establishment regarded itself as highly cosmopolitan, yet was bounded by a Square Mile mentality, an inalienable belief in its own omnicompetence. The past couple of decades have changed all that, and it is people such as Nat West's Bob Alexander who have been the agents of that change. Not that it was an easy job recasting an inherited mindset, as Bob himself discovered.

When I joined Nat West in 1990 the Board was full of old bankers. They laid down the law, and their law was absolute. The few people recruited from outside their magic circle were mostly ex-politicians, who may have been able to open doors in Timbuktu and Basutoland, but had virtually no experience of the cut-and-thrust of the business world. It was a cosy, even incestuous arrangement, and in my early days we off-comers were all too often befuddled by the mysteries that the insiders made of their profession, as the debacle over Nat West Markets revealed.

Run by Dr Martin Owen, and established to tap into the highly complex futures and derivative markets, the operation made a bit of money to begin with, but all too soon it was in serious trouble, yet Nat West continued to pay astronomical sums to Owen's team who, quite simply, were failing to deliver. Indeed, the Board voted very closely to keep the operation going, with disastrous consequences. Eventually, Nat West Markets was shut down, but not before it had cost the Bank almost £100 million. Indeed, important questions still remain to be answered about why the Bank allowed Nat West Markets to continue trading for so long at such a high cost to its business.

Whatever the answer, the debacle reflected as much on the arcane, inner workings of the Bank as on the culture that perpetuated it, and I suspect that it was exactly this, the cultural mindset of the Old Guard, that initially underminded Bob Alexander's efforts to modernize the business. To me, in fact, the saddest thing about the whole, convoluted Nat West Markets affair was that it exposed Bob Alexander to a broadside of criticism, not least, whether he was a fit man to be in charge of the Bank's business. Since my first days in Lothbury it was clear to me that Bob was determined to drag the Nat West into the twentieth, if not the twenty-first century, and I still wonder whether there were elements within the hierarchy who did not take kindly to his radical agenda. Maybe I was imagining things, but it seemed to me that during my first couple of years in Lothbury, I was caught up in a culture-clash between the old and the new. Or perhaps I was right. Perhaps the old prejudice against trade remained, and I was regarded as much as an interloper as a representative of the modernizing tendency that was viewed with grave suspicion by the establishment: 'MacLaurin, good Lord, ain't he a grocer?'

In fact, I suspect that this was at the root of my own reservations about the management of the Bank: that I was a grocer in the people business, rather than a trader in abstractions. From the outset I could never get my mind around the 'Them and Us' attitude that permeated the whole business, shot through, as it was, with arrogance. And there's that word arrogance again, the point and counterpoint of all that I have learned during my time in business. The temptation to get above oneself is always there, of course, as I had to be reminded during my time as Chairman of Tesco. The company had been having a particularly good run and at some dinner or other I said something like: 'Nothing can stop us now'. It was a crazy thing to say. We were becoming too arrogant for our own good, and when the economy ran into a bit of difficulty, and our profits started slowing down, I wasn't allowed to forget my own, ill-judged remark, or the lesson that it taught me: never start to believe that you are bloody fantastic, because you are not.

The trouble with the establishment at Nat West was that they thought they were fantastic, and they treated their own people and their customers accordingly. The contrast with Tesco was extraordinary. Where we maintained a dialogue with our own people and our customers as a matter of company policy, it seemed to me that the hierarchs at the Nat West had little time for either. The world was out there, somewhere, peopled by sundry debtors and creditors, but all safely distanced from the cloistered retreat of Lothbury. Once again it was an attitude that Bob Alexander struggled to change by actively engaging the Bank's staff in discussions about the Nat West's future, but the old prejudices died hard, which may have done something to account for the Bank's rejection of the Clubcard Plus scheme launched by Tesco.

It is easy to explain why Tesco went into Clubcard in 1996. All our customer surveys, all our customer panels were coming through with much the same message: 'We like Tesco very much. You've done a lot that we've suggested by providing wider aisles, and a greater range of fresh foods, and opening more checkouts at busy times, but as regular shoppers who spend a lot in your stores, why can't we have something like an Air Miles scheme to repay us for our loyalty?' No question, we gave the proposal a great deal of thought, and no question, either, we did a lot of research into the idea, but the Clubcard initiative was essentially customer-driven, and the Nat West were only too happy to be involved in the project.

When it came, the launch of Clubcard was an enormous success, thanks largely to the commitment of Tesco's staff. As with Operation Checkout, the whole operation had been kept under wraps until our stores closed on Friday evening and then, in a seventy-two-hour blitz, we explained to them exactly what we were about, and what we were asking of them. And they responded magnificently. Without the goodwill of our staff, in fact, the company would have been hard-pressed to cope with the huge demand to join 'the Club' which, within months, had recruited more than five million Card holders. I don't think that anyone except, that is, for David Sainsbury who dismissed Clubcard as being 'no better than electronic Green Shield stamps', was left in any doubts about the market potential for loyalty cards, least of all the Bank. Indeed, it was the success of the scheme that encouraged Tesco to look more closely at the whole, complex issue of financial services, more especially when our customers began to say: 'Well we've got your Card, and that's fine, but is there some way we can use it to pay for our groceries?'

Again, much of the initiative for Clubcard Plus came from the public, and we approached Nat West to see if they would be interested in an extension of the original scheme. The meeting was held at Lothbury, and I took a team to meet Bob Alexander and his people to talk through the whole idea. Our pitch was quite simple: 'You've done Clubcard with us, and that's going very well, now we'd like to do Clubcard Plus with the Bank'. I, for one, certainly thought it was an offer they couldn't refuse. But there I was wrong. They just didn't want to know, and later I got a letter from Bob saying that he had found himself in an impossible position, and asking somewhat plaintively: 'What could I do?'

It was a question which I was unable to answer. All that I did know, and something which I still believe, is that a continuing association between Tesco and Nat West would have done the Bank a lot of good. As it was, we struck a deal with the Royal Bank of Scotland, and I resigned from the Nat West Board because of the conflict of interests involved. Subsequently, Tesco did have some teething troubles when it launched out into financial services, but I think that this had little to do with Nat West's decision which, I suspect, was once again the product of the Lothbury mindset – the last vestige, hopefully, of the establishment's lingering prejudice against 'trade'.

Not that Nat West was by any means unique. Quite the reverse. As far as I could see, during my early days with the Bank, much of the City was dominated by reach-me-down conventions dating back to God-knows-when. Certainly, there was widespread agreement that things had to change if the City was to retain its position as a key player in the world's financial markets, the difficulty being to slough off the past. I had lived through a quiet revolution at Tesco, but this demanded a revolution of a quite different order of magnitude, though as far as the banks were concerned, and here again, the irony, this meant adopting many of the business practices of the sector they had patronized for so long: trade.

Tesco were by no means alone in exploring the potential of the financial services sector during the early 1990s. Virtually every other UK multiple – not to mention their overseas competitors – was coming to recognize the opportunities that existed in the sector, the more so in light as much of their trading expertise as of their user-friendly image. For too long, banks had patronized their customers. For too long they had opened their doors at 9.30 and closed them again at 3.00. For too long they had worked a five day week, careless of the fact that they were closed at precisely the time when so many people needed them. For too long they were motivated not so much by how they could help their customers, more by what they could make out of them. A mirror-image of the retail approach, it became increasingly clear to companies, such as Sainsbury's and Tesco, that the entire banking establishment was vulnerable to a challenge to their long established hegemony; that the retailers could, indeed, take the financial sector by the tail, which, to a certain extent, is what has happened during the 1990s.

Geographically, it was little more than a costermonger's holler from Well Street market to Lothbury. Conceptually, they were worlds apart, and for all his chutzpah, I doubt whether the young Jack Cohen could ever have envisaged a day when Tesco would be a significant stakeholder in the financial market, that mortgages, insurance and banking would all be a part of Tesco's stock-in-trade. Undoubtedly, the idea would have delighted him, but I can't believe that even his fertile imagination would have grasped the full implications of exactly what the present-day multiples are about: taking on the banking establishment at their own game. Certainly, the banks have done a great deal to improve their image over the past five years, nonetheless, they've still got some way to go before they become user-friendly, and in this connection they can be sure of one thing: that having secured a bridgehead in the financial sector, retailers will be keen to extend it.

Which raises an interesting question. Could it be that the future gameplan of retailers and banks will lead to mega-mergers between the two? To date, it is a prospect that retail analysts have failed to detect. Once, when the majority of analysts were little better than bystanders at company AGMs, this would not have been so surprising. Today, it is very different. Communications is now the name of the game, which is why most companies now make a practice of setting aside time to brief the new and highly sophisticated generation of analysts that have emerged in the past couple of decades on what they are about, and why, for there is nothing that the City hates more than being taken by surprise. In fact, analysts rarely attend AGMs these days, though their absence is more than compensated for by the growing interest that shareholders take in their holdings, and properly so. It's only right that managements should have to account for their actions to their investors, though there are times when it seems that shareholders are more concerned to close the business than to quiz managements about their performance, and my mind goes back to the first occasion on which I chaired a Tesco AGM in 1986.

The venue was the Savoy, and the meeting itself was comparatively trouble-free. Then came the break for refreshments, and the waiters entered carrying silver salvers full of delicacies – canapés, vol-au-vents, petits fours – shoulder high. What came next was extraordinary. Our shareholders descended like locusts, emptying trays into Tesco carrier bags. Within minutes, the only people left in the room were the Tesco Board and the waiters. As for our shareholders, having cleaned the place out, they had retired to the Embankment Gardens to have a picnic in the sun! The Savoy management was not amused, and the following day I received a brief note saying in so many words: 'Thank you for your custom, but please don't come back again'.

At another Tesco AGM, I had to break up a confrontation between two irate, and elderly gentlemen. Each was clinging to the end of a French bread stick, and roaring at the other: 'I saw it first! It's mine!' 'Liar, I got there first! It's mine.' As tempers flared, the room fell silent until, Solomon-like, I broke the baguette in two, and gave each of them a half share.

Small wonder that analysts now give such functions a wide berth. After all, they've got better things to do with their time, if only to ponder the $64,000 question as to whether there is any likelihood of future mergers taking place between the banking and retail sectors. If they do, indeed, have so much in common, could it be to the advantage of both to combine? A far-fetched notion? Possibly, but then one should never say never. God knows, it's only a few years since the Saatchi brothers made a bid for the Midland Bank, while more recent experience has shown that far from being incompatible the two sectors frequently complement one another, retailers providing the banks with a network of user-friendly outlets through which to do business; banks providing retailers with the expertise necessary to trade in an increasingly complex, global market.

Arguably, in fact, the two are on convergent courses, and maybe one of these days you will find Tesco bidding for the National Westminster Bank. If so, and if my mother was still alive, I suspect it would even do something to temper her prejudice against trade.

CHAPTER SEVEN

A Small Case of Guinness

> For six months, a cabal at Guinness had conspired to deceive, and they very nearly got away with it ... Whoever it was ... who first insisted that Saunders recruit his 'five Scots', it was the non-executive team appointed in the autumn of 1986 who rescued Guinness from total collapse. An exaggeration? Not so.

WHEN I WAS young, there was a famous poster which proclaimed 'Guinness is good for you'. The notion intrigued me. What was this stuff, this Guinness, that the rosy-cheeked character in the sixteen-sheet poster seemed to be enjoying so much? Why, precisely, was it good for *me*? Or anyone else for that matter? It was one of the myriad mysteries of childhood, and all those years ago I could never have imagined that one day, in the autumn of 1986, my car-phone would ring as I was on a business-as-usual trip to a Tesco store and: 'The name's Ernest Saunders. I'm the MD of Guinness. We're looking for five Scots to join the Board. Would you let your name go forward?'

The mystery was as much in the question, as in its preamble. Why, for heaven's sake, five Scots? What had Scottishness to do with being on the Board of Guinness? In the months ahead – months during which the 'Guinness Affair' dominated the headlines – I was to learn at least some of the answers, and the more I learned, the more I wondered what *good* Guinness was doing for the reputation of those blue-chip institutions that were so deeply involved with it. For Guinness was more than one of those questionable deals that rocked the City in the mid-1980s. In the *Daily Mirror*'s terms it was 'The Big 'Un', and it was one of my fellow 'Scots' – and being only half Scottish, I used the word circumspectly – who was later to summarize the convoluted affair.

Ian Chapman is a no-nonsense businessman, as Scottish and canny as they come. A brilliant publisher, whose lists have included a shelfful of top-selling authors, he is not a man given to hyperbole, but when he reflected at the close of the affair that: 'If anyone had come up with a manuscript based on the case, I'd have told them that I didn't deal in fantasy,' I knew precisely what he meant. In retrospect, the whole thing was fantastic, a cat's-cradle of intrigue which, as it unravelled, convulsed the entire business world. Not that I had any inkling of what was to come when I stalled Saunders' invitation, for there were some big questions to be asked before reaching a decision, not least: Why me? Was it simply that my name sounded Scottish, or was there more to it than that? Had he simply been playing lucky-dip with all the Mac's in *Who's Who*, all sixty pages of them, or was he playing a deeper game?

True, I knew something of the background to the recent Guinness takeover of United Distillers, and true, I'd heard rumours that the Edinburgh financial establishment, the so-called 'Charlotte Square mafia', had been none-too-happy with the outcome. Nonetheless, the question remained: Why me? As one of Tesco's major suppliers, I knew something of the long and distinguished history of Guinness, but little beyond that, and for twenty-four hours I pondered Saunders' invitation, and wondered exactly what it implied. And what of Saunders himself? His reputation certainly preceded him, for there could be no question that he had done an outstanding job for Guinness since being appointed the company's Managing Director in 1981. Indeed, he was widely regarded as the White Knight who had saved the company from itself, or rather, from the Guinness family.

Much like Tesco, in fact, the Guinness establishment had outlived their time, and by the late 1970s the company was widely regarded as nearing its sell-by date. For more than a decade its core business, brewing, had been performing erratically, though its non-brewing activities in property, plastics and confectionery had tended to disguise the full extent of the problem. Indeed, the *Investors' Chronicle* was confident enough to predict in January 1979, that: 'Diversification is good for Guinness'. Its optimism was short-lived. In less than a year, as the company's share price fell, the word in the City was that the best hope for Guinness lay in being taken over. Then Ernest Saunders arrived.

A marketing man, first with a background with J. Walter Thompson, and later with Schweppes and Beechams, he had enhanced his already powerful reputation by the way he had handled a crisis in his former company, Nestlé. Charged with hard-selling unsuitable baby foods in the Third World, a charge which led the World Food Organization to boycott Nestlé products, Saunders recruited a panel of doctors to refute the allegation, which allowed Nestlé time to clean up its act. The record was an impressive one, and it was to be fortified by his performance at Guinness. Within a couple of years of his arrival, Saunders had restructured the company's management, and entered the takeover trail – a combination that was to have far-reaching consequences.

At the time, however, the arrival on the scene of Thomas Ward, an American lawyer, and a long-time friend of Saunders, and Olivier Roux, an employee of Bain, a management consultancy, who had been seconded to Guinness as its Financial Director, caused little comment. City-watchers had better things to do with their time than to speculate on why Saunders should create a team of insider/outsiders at the heart of the business, the more so as Guinness appeared to be hellbent on the acquisition trail, absorbing first, Martins the newsagents, and then in quick succession, Champneys health farm, the Seven-Eleven retail group, and Richters, the food importers.

Apparently, growth by acquisition was where the action lay, and in June 1985, the company made a bid for Bells, the Scottish distillers. Significantly, much of the Scottish establishment, including Sir Thomas Risk, Chairman of the Bank of Scotland, were bitterly opposed to the idea of a Sassenach takeover of a prized Scottish institution, and one which distilled Scotch whisky at that! It used to be said that a Scot will not fight until he sees the sight of his own blood, and if there was blood still to be drawn, there could be no question that with Guinness' bid for Bells, the blood of the Charlotte Square mafia was roused.

The contest for control of Bells was hard-fought and bitter, but in the late summer of 1985, Guinness clinched the deal with a bid of £370 million, but not before there was talk that the Chairman of Guinness' bankers, Morgan Grenfell, had been economical with the truth about his involvement in the takeover, and that the Stock Exchange had investigated rumours of insider trading. Little more than a whisper it soon became the loudest whisper of them all.

Like so many companies at the time, Distillers, a dominant player in the whisky business, was suffering from management fatigue, and as Guinness had recently been, it was vulnerable to a takeover bid. Although first established in the 1920s, it seemed at times as if the Distillers' Board was caught up in a time warp with their lush offices and their opulent lifestyle. It was Jimmy Gulliver, the Chairman of Argyll, who first recognized Distillers' weaknesses, and made the first move in what was to become the tangled story of the Guinness Affair.

In December 1985, Argyll bid 485p a share for Distillers, but although Gulliver was a Scot, born and bred, the Distillers' Board wanted nothing of him, one of their directors remarking: 'Gulliver deals in potatoes and cans of beans. We are selling Scotch'. As contemptuous as it was patronizing, the aside was a measure of the mindset of the Distillers' Board. Seemingly, it was a case of 'Anyone but Argyll', and Guinness was happy to oblige. Since the previous autumn, Guinness had been exploring the possibilities of making a bid for Distillers, but now it was Distillers that was to approach Guinness to explore the possibilities of Guinness mounting a counter bid for the company, a deal that gained in attraction when Sir Thomas Risk accepted Saunders' invitation to become Chairman of the new group if the Guinness bid proved successful. It was one of the two inducements – the other being that Guinness would locate its headquarters in Edinburgh if the merger took place – aimed at allaying Scottish fears that for a second time in less than a year, Scotland would be losing control of one of its most prestigious companies.

A month was to pass between Argyll tabling its offer and Guinness coming in with a counter bid of eight Guinness shares plus £7 in cash for every Distillers' share. It was the beginning of what the *Guardian* was to call 'the financial imbroglio' which was to be played out in public for the next three months – bid and counter bid – whilst in private, deals were done, and secret agreements struck. Inevitably, the intricacies of such mega-mergers are complex, but in this case they were compounded by the complexity of the network of advisers and consultants that Saunders had assembled around him – advisers and consultants who, in the aftermath, were as quick to distance themselves from the affair, as they were to collect their fees. Whatever the cost, however, it seemed as if this was one contest that Saunders' ego would not allow him to lose. There was too much of his vanity at stake for that, and as the in-fighting intensified, and rumours of sleaze began to circulate, Guinness continued to raise its game until, in mid-April, it controlled a majority shareholding in Distillers. The battle had been won. The inquest was about to begin.

Indeed, Saunders' euphoria must have been short-lived, partly as a result of his own duplicity. Within a week of closing the deal for Distillers, he had reneged on both his undertakings to the Distillers' Board. Sir Thomas Risk was not to replace Lord Iveagh as Chairman of the newly formed group, and London, not Edinburgh, would remain the headquarters of the new conglomerate. The Charlotte Square mafia was incensed. They made dangerous enemies, and they were not alone. In the City there were growing suspicions about exactly what had occurred during the Guinness takeover; growing doubts about Saunders and his advisers' role in the affair, suspicions and doubts that were to be reinforced when it was revealed, in early June, that during a visit to the States, Saunders had invested $100 million of Guinness capital in an investment fund run by Ivan Boesky. A junk bond dealer who lived by his maxim 'Greed is Good', Boesky had already been identified as an insider trader by the US authorities when the deal with Guinness was struck, and it was their evidence that was to alert the Department of Trade and Industry that there might well have been something seriously amiss with the Distillers deal.

Which was when I received my call from Ernest Saunders: 'We're looking for five Scots to join the Board. Would you let your name go forward?' I wasn't the only one to receive the invitation, and it was only later that I learned why Saunders had been so anxious to recruit a new team of independent executives. Seemingly, the Bank of England was increasingly concerned about Saunders' burgeoning power within Guinness, whilst as a result of the American tip-off, the DTI was threatening to hold an inquiry into the takeover of Distillers. A formidable combination, they posed a serious threat to Saunders, and it was only when he agreed to appoint five outsiders to the Board that the DTI postponed its decision to investigate the company's affairs. Originally, only four of us were appointed: Sir Norman Macfarlane, Chairman of Clansman; Sir David Plastow, Chief Executive of Vickers; Tony Greener, Managing Director of Dunhills, and myself, to be joined later by Ian Chapman, the Chairman and Chief Executive of Collins.

To say the least, the Scottish connections of the group were tenuous, only two of the five having close Scottish links. Whatever the case, however, I suspect that our appointments not only satisfied the Bank and the DTI, albeit temporarily, but also served Saunders' end in his continuing efforts to assuage the Charlotte Square mafia. As for myself, I spent a day pondering his invitation before deciding to accept, ignorant as much of the background to the situation as to what it would involve. I was soon to learn. Saunders was later to say that he found it 'quite thrilling to interview these famous people'. The feeling was far from mutual.

No question, the Saunders I met on my first visit to the Guinness headquarters was charm personified. All the polish, all the panache of the marketing man that he had once been was there: a slightly bent figure, grey haired, softly spoken, but vain, the sort of character who preens himself in whatever mirror he happens to be passing, and insists on taking the table facing the door in restaurants so that he can see and be seen by the clientele. But what of Saunders himself, the man who had masterminded one of the largest takeovers on record? The answers came soon enough. When I asked if I could have copies of recent minutes, he said that he never kept any. When I requested a sight of any records he held of meetings with his executive team, he explained that he held a weekly meeting with those concerned, but they went unreported. And when I pressed him for details of the company's recent history, not least of its dealings with Distillers, he referred me to Olivier Roux.

Saunders' attitude astonished me. How was it possible to run a company like Guinness without keeping any records, any minutes? Why was he being so secretive? What, exactly, lay behind the bland exterior, the charm, the panache? Was Saunders simply a reflection of the arcane nature of Guinness's management style, or did he have something to hide? Apparently, Olivier Roux could provide some of the answers, and together with Tony Greener I visited his office in Portman Square. Even then I couldn't get a handle on how it was that the Finance Director of Guinness was still on the payroll of Bain, the management consultants, and our briefing did little to reassure me that we'd heard the full story of the recent history of Guinness. All that became clear, in fact, was that Saunders had made a mystery of the management of the company; a conjuror whose sleight of hand defied the eye of the ordinary punter.

The meeting with Roux lasted for four hours, and when we left I suggested to Tony Greener that it would be useful to discuss what we had learned over an early lunch at the nearby Portman Hotel. I remember nothing of that meal, which is hardly surprising. We had other, more important things on our minds, not least, what we had just heard. Superficially, it had all sounded plausible enough, but we sensed that there was more to it than Roux had been willing to reveal, and if so, what lay beneath the gloss that he had placed on events? What was it that he was trying to hide? The answers eluded us. All that we sensed was that there was something wrong at Guinness. And our two fellow, non-executive directors – Sir Norman Macfarlane and Sir David Plastow – agreed. Something was seriously wrong in Portman Square, but exactly what, we had still to discover. We didn't have long to wait.

On 1 December 1986, the DTI moved into Portman Square, armed with authority to investigate the affairs of the company under two sections of the Companies Act. The timing couldn't have been less propitious, for that evening Guinness was to hold a reception in the National Portrait Gallery. All the great and the good had been invited, but as Brian Baldock, then a Director of Guinness, and now a non-executive director of M&S, remembers: 'It was surprising how many people discovered their wives had been taken ill, or their cars had broken down, or that "something urgent had cropped up"'. The excuses thinned the guest list in proportion to the attendance of the press, but while Saunders ducked and wove his way through their questioning that night, he was not to have such an easy passage at a Board meeting the following day. Norman Macfarlane pressed him hard on why the DTI had launched an investigation into the company, and for details of Guinness's dealings with Boesky, I shared his concern: 'Look, Ernest, before we deal with any other business, let me ask you a question: "Is there any reason why the DTI and the Serious Fraud Office should be interested in your own or Guinness's affairs?"'

Saunders' reply was unhesitating: 'Absolutely nothing'.

For a second time I put it to him: 'Then why are they here? Is there anything you want to tell us, because from this moment on we have to take a very different view of affairs?'

And for a second time, Saunders denied, vehemently, that any improprieties had occurred: 'I can assure you and the other non-executive directors that there is nothing I know of that could cause the interest of the DTI and the SFO'.

It was as barefaced as that, and I still wonder what we would have done if Saunders had come clean at that meeting. How would we have reacted if he'd said: 'Look, I've done this that and the other, but we've taken over this fantastic company, Distillers, and I want your support.' As it was, we could only accept his word that there was, indeed, nothing to hide. Within the month, Saunders' word was to be exposed for what it was – worthless. An exponent of the theory that if you're going to tell a lie, then tell a big one and stick to it, he brazened out all accusations of impropriety, and in the belief that defence was the best form of attack, went as far as to try and enlist Mrs Thatcher's support for his cause:

Dear Prime Minister,

May I respectfully draw to your attention the issues of natural justice arising from the actions of the Parliamentary Under Secretary of State and Industry, by his institution . . . of an enquiry into the affairs of Guinness PLC . . . I am concerned that the procedures of an investigation of this kind should establish the facts before any judgement is passed . . . May I ask you . . . to take a personal interest in this matter which raises important legal issues . . . including procedural issues which concern individual freedoms and human rights and the balance between those rights and the power of the state . . . Someone will have to stand up for individual rights in this case. May I ask that it should be you?

Natural justice! Individual freedoms! Human rights! Saunders made a play of the words, and as the whole labyrinthine intrigue began to unravel, and the net closed inexorably around him, he was to become increasingly paranoid. With the DTI inspectors in Portman Square, he moved out to a suite in the Inn on the Park, the first of a series of moves induced by his fear that wherever he settled he was being bugged, that people were actively plotting against him. Little by little the man was cracking up under the pressure, though the five non-executives had still to appreciate the ramifications of the operation he had masterminded. A conspiratorial mosaic, the pieces only fell into place in piecemeal order in the early days of our enquiry: the fact that Guinness had paid £180 million in fees to advisers and consultants in 1985–86; evidence that on one occasion during the takeover a major transfer of funds had passed through the hands of twenty banks in less than thirty-six hours. What had once been only vague suspicions were slowly being realized, to be reinforced when Saunders decided to take on Sir David Napley, one of Britain's most eminent criminal lawyers, as Guinness's solicitor.

Why? Surely Guinness had no need of a criminal lawyer if there was nothing to hide, for as Brian Baldock asserted at the time: 'if . . . the media became aware that the company had retained Kingsley Napley, it was likely that the inference would be drawn that the company was in some trouble and had . . . retained Sir David because of his reputation in criminal legal matters'. Brian's objection was swept aside. Rather than reassuring the non-executives, however, it merely fuelled them. And there were others who shared our concern. Or, more precisely, were concerned at what might be uncovered. Nothing had been seen of Olivier Roux since early December, and as the investigation gained momentum he had become increasingly anxious about his own role in the affair. Together with Thomas Ward, who had already quit the country, Roux's defection left Saunders isolated. If not his only confidant, Roux had been one of those closest to him. Now their desertion heightened his paranoia.

Inexorably, the whole, carefully constructed edifice of deceit was collapsing around him, though no one yet appreciated how quickly it would occur, and in the week after Christmas, I decided to take time off from the interminable round of meetings at Guinness – at one stage we were meeting for four or five hours a night discussing what was going on – in the fond belief that little would happen during the post-Christmas period. How wrong I was. On 30 December, Roger Seelig, a key player in the affair, resigned from Morgan Grenfell, Guinness's principal banker, amidst rumours of questionable share dealing. It was to trigger a chain reaction.

On New Year's Eve I was in Hong Kong when Mike Darnell phoned me – it was two in the morning Hong Kong time – and said that the word was that the Guinness Affair was brewing up, and that I had better be prepared to come home. It seemed a long way to go for just a couple of days, so I phoned Sir Norman Macfarlane, who held my power of attorney, and asked whether I should return. His answer reassured me: 'There's no need for that. Go off to Australia, and if anything happens I'll give you a call'.

Which I did, to find that when I got to my hotel room in Sydney the message light was flashing: Would I call Tony Greener immediately. When I finally got through, Tony was insistent: 'All hell's breaking loose. You've got to get the next flight back. There's a critical meeting at Millbank and we want you there'. The next flight left for London that evening, and for the next few hours I enjoyed an afternoon's cricket at the Sydney ground, before chasing back the hours to arrive in Heathrow the following morning. Tony met me there, and on the drive into London briefed me on all that had happened in the previous forty-eight hours. It was explosive stuff.

On 4 January, Olivier Roux had finally broken down, and delivered an eight page letter to Sir David Napley, with a copy to Sir Norman Macfarlane. A subjective, but nonetheless highly detailed account of the Guinness Affair, this was whistle-blowing on a grand scale, and it was only when the five non-executives recovered from the first shock of Roux's exposé that they grasped the full extent of Saunders' duplicity, of the fact that he had lied to them not once, but times beyond recall. Listing eleven banks, institutions and individuals whose support Saunders had enlisted during the takeover battle for Distillers – among them some of the best known names in the City – they had been at the heart of an operation which, in the weeks before the takeover, had inflated the price of Guinness's shares by as much as 18 per cent, thus making the company's offer for Distillers that much more attractive to Distillers' shareholders.

Even now, I find it hard to get my head around the sums involved: that during the bid period the 'supporters' recruited by Saunders and his cronies bought seventy-eight million Guinness shares, a quarter of the company's issued capital, at a cost of £257 million. But if the sums slushing around in the world markets – for this was a global operation – were astronomical, they paled in comparison with the Machiavellian nature of the operation itself. Which was precisely what Saunders and his confidants intended. Like the high rollers they were, the main players held their cards close to their chests, and the more complex the game, the more secretive they became until they, too, lost track of who, precisely, was calling the shots – Saunders, Thomas Ward or the motley collection of banks and individuals who each had taken a stake in the gamble. Small wonder that Saunders kept so few records, for he did, indeed, have a finesse to hide, a hand to bluff Distillers' shareholders into believing that Guinness was good for them.

In fact, it was to take the Inspectors appointed by the DTI – an eminent barrister and an equally eminent accountant – more than a decade to disentangle the web of deception that made headlines of the Guinness Affair, for them to conclude:

Though our sensibilities may have been numbed by long confrontation with the evidence, three features still shine disturbingly through . . . from the detail of our findings. Firstly, the cynical disregard of laws and regulations; secondly, the cavalier misuse of company monies; thirdly, a contempt for truth and common honesty: all these in a part of the City which was thought respectable.

Their indictment was damning, though the five non-execs had little idea of the full extent of the scam before we had sight of the Roux letter. Carefully worded as it was, there was no disguising his intentions, to exculpate himself by shopping his former colleagues (Roux was later to turn Queen's Evidence), and it certainly explained some of the mysteries surrounding the Distillers deal, not least, Guinness's $100 million investment in Boesky's slush fund. By January 1987, Boesky, the model for the asset-stripping anti-hero in Oliver Stone's movie *Wall Street*, was already beginning a three-year sentence for insider trading, though no mention of the Guinness Affair was made during the court hearing. As far as Sir Norman Macfarlane and the rest of the 'Scots directors' were concerned, in fact, the full details of Boesky's involvement in the Distillers takeover only came to light as a result of Roux's letter.

In April 1986, as the battle for Distillers was reaching its climax, Ward and Saunders lunched with Gerald Ronson, Chairman and Chief Executive of Heron International, at Portman Square. Ronson, who was himself already deeply involved in the affair, having purchased eight million Guinness shares at a cost of £27 million, on the guarantee of indemnification for his support during the operation, was asked by Ward whether he knew of a good man to do business with in the States. Ronson did: Ivan Boesky. After handing over Boesky's New York phone number, Ronson agreed to speak to Boesky and alert him to expect a call from Guinness. Within a fortnight Boesky had purchased twelve million Guinness shares, 4 per cent of the company's share capital at a cost of £41 million. He was not in business for charity's sake, however. He wanted his kick-backs, and within days of the close of the Distillers bid, discussions began as to how Guinness could 'reimburse' Boesky, culminating in a breakfast meeting between Saunders, Ward and Boesky in New York.

The situation verged on the farcical. Unbeknown to Saunders or Ward, Boesky had already struck a deal with the US authorities to monitor conversations with his business contacts, and he may well have been wired for sound during the meeting on 15 May. If so, if Federal agents were, indeed, plugged into the conspirators' discussions, it may well have been what alerted them and, subsequently, the DTI to Boesky's involvement in the Guinness Affair. Whatever the case, Guinness invested $100 million in Ivan Boesky & Company LP within ten days of that breakfast meeting – a pay-off which the DTI Inspectors were later to describe as 'indefensible'.

Roux's letter did much more than implicate Boesky in the scam, however. In a passing reference to Boesky, it also fingered an altogether more significant player in the affair: Bank Leu of Zurich, at that time one of the five largest Swiss banks. Eight years had passed since Saunders quite Nestlé, but he still retained contact with Dr Artur Furer, one-time Chairman of the company. Indeed, in 1983, and largely at Saunders' instigation, Furer had been appointed a non-executive director of Guinness, a year before he became Supervisory Chairman of Bank Leu. As early as 1985, Furer had been involved in a deal under which the Bank would have provided Guinness with a £10 million loan in order to buy shares during its takeover bid for Bells. The deal came to nothing, but as the DTI report noted: 'This ungerminated seed was . . . to display interesting fecundity during the bid for Distillers'.

As Roux's letter was to reveal. If he was to be believed, Saunders and Ward, with Furer's connivance, had arranged for

Bank Leu to extend two lines of credit to Guinness: one of £75 million to buy 3 per cent of Distillers' stock; the other of £50 million to purchase Guinness shares. In effect, Guinness was buying shares in itself to inflate their price and fool the unsuspecting during the final stages of the contest for Distillers. If proved, Roux's charges against Saunders and Ward were ruinous, the trouble not only being that they remained unsubstantiated, but also that they were levelled by a man who, himself, had been deeply involved in the whole affair. The question was: What should the Board do? How should they respond? Could they rely on Roux's evidence, and if so, should they sack Saunders or merely suspend him? And what did Saunders himself have to say in his own defence?

The answers, when they came, were, to say the least, unhelpful. At 3.00 p.m. on 6 January, nine Guinness directors met at Sir David Napley's office, for Sir Norman Macfarlane to tax Saunders on the contents of Roux's letter. He flatly denied the allegations it contained, saying that it was the first that he had heard of them. Momentarily, there was an impasse, then Roux was called in and repeated his charge that a massive cover-up had taken place during the Guinness Affair. Who was to be believed – Roux who, as Sir David Napley pointed out, had already implicated himself in the swindle, or the putative defendant, Ernest Saunders? Unless further evidence was forthcoming, more especially of the role that Bank Leu had played in the affair, the stalemate was complete. It was one man's word against another's, and suspicions surrounded both. The only way out was for Guinness's accountants, Price Waterhouse, to conduct a high speed enquiry into precisely what had gone on between Saunders, Ward and Bank Leu during the takeover of Distillers.

And, meanwhile, the question remained: What of Saunders and Roux? Should they be suspended or fired? Significantly, Sir

Norman Macfarlane and the other non-executives present were all for demanding Saunders' resignation. With the exception of Brian Baldock, the rest of the Board disagreed. Saunders should remain, at least temporarily. The divide was as revealing as it was foregone, the more so as far as the Guinness family was concerned. Indeed, the following day, Sir Norman received a quite extraordinary letter from Lord Iveagh, who had not even been present at the meeting:

> I have reluctantly come to the view that the newly appointed members of the non-executive committee appear to be more concerned with the interests of their group, rather than the interest of the Company's shareholders and the price, and if any adverse public statements are made the newly appointed members of the non-executive committee must bear full responsibility for any adverse effects upon the Company – its share price, its liability to legal action by other parties, and its overall trading interest. It is with regret that I have to say that the manner in which you are conducting the affairs of the non-executive committee have led me to lose confidence in you as chairman of that committee.

It was not the only note that Macfarlane received. Two other family members – Jonathan and Edward Guinness – wrote to him in much the same vein. What they implied was, frankly, mind-boggling. Only four months had passed since Saunders' 'five Scots' had joined the Board, yet now it appeared as if we were being held responsible for the crisis at Guinness; that rather than Saunders or Roux or the Guinness family, it was the five non-executive directors who, in their own interests, were threatening the interests of the company which they had been appointed to oversee. It seemed that the world, or at least that part of it that revolved around Portman Square, was being turned upside down: that it was we who were now in the dock, not those who had been responsible for the debacle.

The notion mocked reason. Inverted as the logic was, however, it was at least partly comprehensible in the family's terms. Saunders had, indeed, been the White Knight who had saved the company from itself; who, having averted the danger of Guinness being taken over, had masterminded a series of takeovers that had re-established Guinness as a major player in the drinks industry. Although control of the business had slipped away from them (Jonathan Guinness was to entitle his book on the subject *Requiem for a Family Business*), I suspect that the Guinnesses nonetheless felt if not a debt of loyalty, then of gratitude to Saunders for all that he had done for the family's fortunes. So much, of course, is speculation, though it does something to explain Lord Iveagh's letter. Not that he, or the family, could avert the now imminent crisis.

On Friday 9 January, the *Evening Standard* led with the headlines SAUNDERS MUST GO, and at 9.00 p.m. that evening he resigned. For five days the media had laid siege to the Guinness headquarters, while the crisis was discussed behind closed doors. Now the news was out. Even then, however, Saunders managed to place a spin on the reason for his departure: 'I feel personally that because of the uncertainty and disruption that has been caused to the business as a result of the Department of Trade and Industry inquiry, this action should be in the best interests of the company, its shareholders, its employees and my family'. Never explain. Never apologize. To the last, Saunders remained a marketing man, although a weekend meeting in Switzerland with Artur Furer must have convinced him that if he had not jumped, he would most certainly have been pushed.

Since early in the previous week, Price Waterhouse had been

conducting an intensive inquiry into the exact nature of Bank Leu's dealings with Guinness. Their report was completed by the 12th, and it was damning. In the dry-as-dust fashion of accountants they revealed that in April 1986, Pipetec AG, a subsidiary of Bank Leu, had 'upon respective instructions received from yourself' (T. J. Ward) bought Distillers shares to the value of £75,612,149.38p. And this was only the tip of the intrigue. In June 1986, a wholly-owned subsidiary of Guinness, G&C Moore Limited, whose investment portfolio was managed by Sir Jack Lyons, had deposited £50 million with Bank Leu (Luxembourg), two months after Bryton A-G, yet another, wholly-owned subsidiary of Bank Leu, had agreed 'on the instructions of T. J. Ward ... to purchase Guinness shares to the aggregate value of up to £50 million'.

In short, Guinness, with the connivance of Bank Leu, had created a false market in Guinness shares contrary not only to the City Code of Takeovers and Mergers but also to the Companies Act. Nothing is known of what Saunders and Furer discussed during their weekend meeting in Geneva. Only one thing, in fact, is certain: that both men must have known that their financial shenanigans were about to be exposed, and that they could no longer conceal the Bank's involvement in the Guinness Affair. Or, in Saunders' case, the questions of the 'astronomic sums' (a phrase that occurs and reoccurs in the Inspectors' final report) that were paid out by Guinness for 'services rendered' to the sundry advisers and consultants assembled by Saunders' team in return for their support during the company's contest for Distillers, amongst others:

- £330,000 to Sir Jack Lyons, to be 'buried' in a US account
- £880,000 to L. F. Rothschild for 'advice and research'

- £1.1 million to Erlanger and Co. for 'work in connection with the acquisition of Distillers'
- £1.6 million to Morgan Grenfell and its subsidiary Morgan Grenfell Laurie for confidential market support on operations
- £2.5 million to Gerald Ronson's company, Heron International, for 'services rendered', and a further 'present' of $4.8 million to one of Heron's US subsidiaries, the Pima Service Corporation
- £3.3 million to Anthony Parnes, negotiated by Sir Jack Lyons as a 'corporate success fee'
- £5.2 million to Thomas Ward's company, Marketing and Acquisition Consultants, for: 'Advice in relation to strategy and execution in respect of the successful acquisition of Distillers PLC'

Virtually all the above sums were repaid either immediately before, or immediately after the Guinness scandal broke. In revealing the cost of the support 'bought' by Guinness during the takeover, however, the figures disguise the convoluted nature of many of the subsequent pay-offs. For instance, the £5.2 million fee to Marketing and Acquisition Consultants passed through sixteen UK, Channel Island, Swiss, Austrian and US banks before being credited to Ward's account in Maryland. And even that was not the end of the tortuous trail, for as the DTI Inspectors subsequently discovered, the £5.2 million credited to Ward had passed through Ernest Saunders' Swiss bank account. No wonder that as latecomers to the company, Sir Norman and the rest of the non-executives found it virtually impossible to disentangle the web that Saunders and his cronies had woven around their dealings, or that it took the Inspectors more than a decade to complete their inquiry.

For six months, a cabal at Guinness had conspired to deceive, and they very nearly got away with it. Indeed, it was absurd for Lord Iveagh to suggest that it was the new non-executives who were responsible for the debacle of January 1987. Whoever it was, the Bank of England, the Scottish Office, the DTI, or a combination of all three, who first insisted that Saunders recruit his 'five Scots', it was the non-executive team appointed in the autumn of 1986 who rescued Guinness from total collapse. An exaggeration? Not so. It was their suspicions about what they discovered – or more exactly, what they had been prevented from discovering – during their short time in Portman Square that fortified the authorities' belief that Saunders and his cronies had been party to a massive fraud.

I'm fortunate enough to have been a non-executive director of a number of companies – Enterprise Oil, National Westminster, Whitbread, Vodafone – but my time at Guinness must rank as the most extraordinary experience I've ever had. Of course, that's easy enough to say in retrospect. At the time it was very different. At the time it seemed as if the five non-executives were caught up in a crisis from which there was no escape, a kind of black hole in the Guinness universe, and it was only due to the way in which Sir Norman, now Lord Macfarlane, led the non-executive team that Guinness came through the other side. No wonder the Guinness family were so hostile to him. Dissimulation had no place in his book. What he was after was the truth, and careless of protocol, he concentrated the minds of his team to discover precisely what had been going on in Portman Square.

In fact, if any one episode in my business career was to convince me of the value of non-executives, it was the Guinness Affair – provided that they don't regard the role as a soft option. And there was no danger of that as far as David Plastow, Tony Greener, and Ian Chapman were concerned. For four months they devoted themselves to confirming their instincts that something was, indeed, wrong with Guinness – and the following year in sorting out the mess that Saunders had left behind. Which, in itself, was a formidable undertaking. The whole enterprise had been painstakingly designed to deceive, and I sometimes wonder whether the Guinness Affair would ever have been exposed for the conspiracy that it was if the conspirators had had access to the advanced systems that are available today.

I recently heard a high-tech boffin discussing the emergent problems of the technology in which he is engaged, more especially, of its potential to disguise both the sources and the destinations of financial transactions, and the consequent danger of major, financial transfers being 'lost' on the now globalized, technological networks. He ended on an up-beat note, that Internet transfers could help to democratize the financial markets, but not before reflecting that it was impossible to legislate against corruption. My mind went back to that day when Ernest Saunders resigned. What if he, and his fellow conspirators, had been able to exploit the extraordinary potential of the systems that are now operational? God knows, they had tried hard enough to disguise the extent of their duplicity, but what if they had been able to 'lose' all evidence of the fraudulent dealings that had taken place? Would the Guinness Affair have ever been exposed? The question is in the past tense, and can never be answered. But what of today? What if a new generation of fraudsters, descendants of men such as Boesky and Ward, but now armed with advanced systems, should emerge to play the global markets in the certainty that it will be virtually impossible to keep track of their chicanery?

The scenario has a certain nightmare quality, or maybe the

fact is that I'm a technological pessimist. If so, I can at least console myself with the thought that smart systems are only as smart as the characters who operate them, and ultimately it was human fallibility that led to Saunders' downfall, and the exposé of the Guinness Affair. At one of the innumerable trials and appeals at which he appeared, on charges ranging from conspiracy to false accounting, from breaches of the Companies Act to theft, Saunders was to assert that he had a very limited involvement in Guinness's bid for Distillers, having left 'Matters of a financial nature relating to the bid . . . to those far more experienced than I . . .'.

Who was he attempting to fool, if not himself? Yet perhaps that was the essence of the man. Perhaps Saunders, the quintessential marketing man, had been sucked into the vortex of deception that became known as the Guinness Affair, to the point where he began to believe in his own lies. Perhaps, once committed, he found that there could be no turning back, and that as the lies multiplied he became trapped by the conspiracy he had created. In the autumn of 1986 when Saunders had phoned me, I had wondered who he was. Paradoxically, the more I learned about him, the less I seemed to know of the man himself: the White Knight of Guinness who came close to destroying the company he had saved.

What was it that motivated him? For seventeen days he stood in the dock at Southwark Crown Court but the enigma remained: questions not so much about Saunders' secrets, more of the secret of Saunders himself, a man who at one time appeared to have everything, only to destroy himself. Was it simply that he, too, subscribed to Boesky's credo 'Greed is Good', or was Saunders more complex than that, as complex, in fact, as the fraud he engineered? If, indeed, he is incapable of distinguishing truth from falsehood then I'll never know.

All that I do know is that poster, glimpsed in childhood – Guinness is Good for You – is no longer a mystery to me. Precisely who it was good for during the crisis that racked the company is difficult to say.

CHAPTER EIGHT

Noblesse Oblige

What has struck me most forcibly about what has been called 'the finest Club in Europe' is the unique concentration of experience to be found in the Upper House, in the arts and education, in the law and in business, in science and medicine, in government itself. You name it, and the expertise is there in the Lords, the problem being to redefine its role and, thus, ensure that it continues to play a constructive role in tomorrow's world.

NOTHING EXCEPTIONAL HAPPENED on the day in 1996 when I was invited to join the Lords, but then what did I expect? The sun to go out, the sky to fall in? The notion was absurd. After all, the Peers had been about their business for longer than most of them cared to remember, and believe me, certain of their Lordships have unconscionably long memories, yet when Lord Strathclyde first asked whether I would be interested in taking a seat in the Upper House, I thought for a moment that perhaps that this was, indeed, some sort of virtual reality then wondered what my mother would have made of it all: Lord MacLaurin of Where or, rather, Wherever. But that was to come later. Much later. Parliamentary procedures are not to be hurried. As I was to discover, there are protocols to be observed, due processes to be solemnized, and I had almost forgotten about that Tuesday lunch with its out-of-the-blue invitation when a call came through on my private line at Tesco.

Ann will tell you that I'm not at my best in the early morning, and 7.45 a.m. office time is certainly not the best of times to call me, especially when the caller is almost as brusque as I feel:

'Cranborne here.'

'Cranborne who?'

'Lord Cranborne. I'm the Conservative Leader in the Lords.'

And as I muttered something about: 'Oh, I'm terribly sorry, but I wasn't expecting to hear from you at quarter-to-eight in the morning,' he reiterated Lord Strathclyde's invitation, whilst I babbled on like a tongue-tied schoolkid: 'Overwhelmed . . . honoured . . . flattered to think . . .'. What he made of it, I can't say. All that I knew was the delight that this was not virtual but reality after all. Then the waiting began all over again. Days passed. Weeks passed. Even time, it seemed, was going slow, and it wasn't until I attended a sports gathering at Number 10, that I heard anything further. There were a couple of hundred people present, but as I was leaving, John Major took me to one side and said: 'Delighted to hear that you feel able to support the Conservatives in the Lords. I'm seeing the Queen next week, and the chances are that you'll be appointed, though I can't say more than that.'

I wandered off into Downing Street wondering what difference it would make to our holiday plans. It was all very well becoming Lord MacLaurin of This, That or the Other, but what of Ann's planned visit to Spain? After all, life's all about priorities, and that August of 1996 our first priority was to get in a few rounds of golf at the Valderrama Club. I was out on the practice range when the General Manager of the Club rushed up, almost incoherent with excitement: 'Ian, Ian, the Prime Minister's on the phone'.

Priorities indeed! I dropped my club and sprinted to take the call: 'Ian. Congratulations. You're going to be working for us in the Lords'.

When he asked if I was having a good holiday, all I could think of to say was: 'I'm about to play the best eighteen holes of my life.' Which I did.

Seemingly, the long wait was over. So much for illusions, for as I soon learned, the formalities had just begun, not least to determine precisely who I should be. Ten years before I'd been plain Ian MacLaurin, then came Sir Ian, but now . . . Now, who the devil was I? The Garter King of Arms has his office in the College of Arms, a quiet backwater of history in the tumult of the City, where he sits ensconced behind a huge desk furnished solely with one of those old-fashioned bells which, once thumped, toll like the proverbial death knell. Or at least, that's how I remember it: the desk, the bell, and the Garter King of Arms, a fantasy figure made real:

'All right, so what kind of title do you have in mind?' and, diffidently, I suggested a Scottish one.

'Impossible. If you were to be granted a Scottish title you'd have to see Lyons up in Edinburgh, and I've already spoken to him, and he tells me that you don't qualify. Next?'

Next? Next? I wondered what, or rather where next? 'Well, I've lived in Knebworth for twenty-six years. Knebworth would be rather nice.'

'Impossible. Lord Cobbold lives in Knebworth, and I think he might be upset if you became Lord MacLaurin of Knebworth. Next?'

'Well, how about Malvern? I want to school there.'

'Quite impossible. You can't have Malvern. Viscount Malvern already sits in the House. Next?'

The situation was becoming critical. I was running out of names. 'Cheshunt then. I've worked there for thirty-eight years.'

And suddenly he roared with laughter: 'Oh, you can have Cheshunt. Anyone can have Cheshunt!' After thirty-eight years I wondered what was so funny about Cheshunt. He continued: 'Knebworth? Knebworth? Tell me a bit more about Knebworth. Where is it?'

So I told him: 'It's on the old A1, and I live on the right side going north, and Lord Cobbold lives on the left side. In fact, you could say that Lord Cobbold represents the rich side of Knebworth, and I represent the poor side.' There wasn't even the flicker of a smile, and I thought: 'I'm digging myself into a hole here,' then all of a sudden he hit the ancient bell and his secretary arrived, to pronounce: 'Ian MacLaurin will be known as Lord MacLaurin of Knebworth.'

'But what of Lord Cobbold?' I asked.

My question did not merit a reply. Having once ordained, a Garter King of Arms is not to be denied: 'I've decided, and it is in my gift. You will be Lord MacLaurin of Knebworth.'

And that was that. No nonsense. No ceremony. Nothing but the fact that at last I knew who I was, and now all that remained to be done was to be Introduced to the House and deliver my maiden speech. I'm not usually nervous about speaking in public, I've done it often enough before, but that day in February 1997, was different, very different. In fact, the palaver that preceded the experience was almost as daunting as the experience itself, as I learned on ringing the Whips' Office:

'If it's OK with you, I would like to make my maiden speech in the forthcoming debate on the City of London.'

The momentary silence rebuked me, then: 'Impossible. Quite impossible. Out of the question.'

Apparently, I'd over-stepped the boundaries if not of propriety, then of procedure, but then, how was I to know any better? Since becoming a peer, no one had troubled to tell me anything about the arcane practices that governed their Lordships' business. I'd been invited to join as a working peer, but as far as the Whips' Office was concerned, I might as well never have existed. When I got there, I wasn't given anything to do. No one sat me down and said: 'Can you do this, that or the other?' and I sometimes wondered why I was there at all. I may be a bit of a workaholic who has always believed that if you are going to do a job you do it well, or don't do it at all, yet there I was, a working peer, gratuitously unemployed.

Some months after I had made my maiden speech, I raised the issue with Lord Strathclyde, and explained that as the Whips' Office had made such little use of my time, I was devoting an increasing amount of it to other activities, my Chairmanship of Vodafone; my non-executive directorship of Whitbread; my Chairmanship of the England and Wales Cricket Board. His reply was significant: 'That's fine. We want people sitting in the House who are involved in the real business world.'

Which was all very well as far as it went, but it certainly didn't go far enough that day I rang the Whips' Office and asked if I could be allowed to make my maiden speech. I can't remember precisely what I said in answer to their dismissive reply. All that I do know is that they finally agreed that I should speak third in the debate on the City. And that, I thought, was it. But there again, I was wrong.

'You know the procedure, I suppose?'

'No,' I confessed.

'Ah yes, well . . .' The pain at my ignorance was palpable: 'Well, the cardinal rules are that you must be humble and funny and make one, key point, all in no more than eight minutes. Quite straightforward really: Humble. Funny. To the point. That OK with you?'

And what could I do but agree? In the days ahead I wrote and rewrote my eight minutes' worth to the extent of rehearsing the thing in my dreams: 'My Lords, the question is not so much whether I am humbly amusing, rather whether I am amusingly humble, for that's surely the point . . .', till the moment of truth arrived and I rose to speak. I suspect most people are a bit nervous when it comes to the crunch, but I've never been so petrified as on that first day when I climbed to my feet in the Lords, the more so as just before I started to speak Margaret Thatcher came in and took the seat immediately in front of me. As if I wasn't humble enough already!

Hansard has the full record of my ordeal: of the humility; of the pleasantry ('Your Lordships may know that I have a responsibility in another Lord's, and I trust that you will join with me in wishing the English side well in their forthcoming Test against New Zealand . . .'); of the key point ('the City of London has already played a real role in helping to confirm Britain's position as the enterprise centre of Europe . . .'), and when I finally sat down all I could think of was: 'Thank God it's over. Now for a cup of tea'. Even in this, however, the rules of the place are absolute – a speaker cannot leave the precincts of Westminster until a debate is over – so I retired to the tea room with Baroness O'Cathain to recover from the experience. It was the best cup of tea of my life, and as we were returning to the Chamber we met Margaret Thatcher coming out: 'Ian, welcome to the Lords. I thought your first contribution was quite excellent. Well done indeed.'

Perhaps the ordeal had been worthwhile after all. Perhaps now I would be given something useful to do. Perhaps a great many things, but so much for wishful thinking. I certainly don't have, and never have had, any ambitions of high office. It takes a certain kind of person to be a professional politician, and I have neither the inclination nor the qualifications to do the job. Nonetheless, I did feel that once I was no longer a titled probationer, the Whips might make some use of what qualifications I did possess. Yet all I did was – nothing. It wasn't so much that I was under utilized. I wasn't utilized at all, and the final indignity came when I learned that there was to be a debate on the future of sport, and that I hadn't even been called to speak!

Surely, as Chairman of the England and Wales Cricket Board, this was one issue on which I was entitled to be heard. Possibly I should have checked on the business of the House more carefully, but this did nothing to gainsay the fact that the Whips' Office hadn't even bothered to tell me that the debate was taking place. I'm not an unduly sensitive chap, but when I heard the news I blew a fuse. What the devil was I doing in the Lords if not to speak up for Lord Strathclyde's real business world? When I taxed the Whips on the issue, they were adamant: 'Sorry, you can't speak.'

'What d'you mean, I can't speak? Are you telling me that as Chairman of the ECB I can't speak in a debate affecting the future of cricket?'

'Yes,' they said, 'that's precisely how it is.' I wasn't being allowed to speak because it was a timed debate and all the slots were filled.

'Well if that's the case, I'm not even going to be in the Chamber because people will think it's nuts if the Chairman of the Board is there and has nothing to say.'

And all they said was: 'Sorry, but that's how it is.' It was only later that I learned that was not how it was. Apparently, the powers-that-be had changed the structure of the debate, so that if I had been in the House I could have spoken, and yet no one even had the courtesy to give me a call. My office is in Division Bell distance of the Lords, four, maybe five hundred yards, and I could have been in the Chamber in a handful of minutes, yet the phone never rang. And that made me bloody angry. It was bad enough being embargoed in the first place, but to learn that I could have spoken if only someone had taken the trouble to give me a call seemed to be quite indefensible.

Which prompted an insidious thought: perhaps there was something, after all, in the talk about the need to reform the Lords. Perhaps the Lords had outlived its usefulness, at least in its present form. Of course, the charge is not new. Like some cockshy of the constitution, the Upper House has been a target for critics since Cromwell declared that 'there will never be a good time in England until we have done away with Lords'. No matter whether it was Lord's or The Lords, his intention was the same. Three centuries on, the terms of reference may have changed, but the question remains: granted that a bicameral legislature is central to our system of government, what role should the Upper House play?

Britain has never had a written constitution, of course. In theory, the notion sounds fine. In practice, it can be enervating which is why, pragmatic as always, we have opted for an evolutionary approach to constitutional reform, recognizing that, as in so much else, the ability to adapt to new conditions is the keystone to survival. Two centuries ago, Edmund Burke, one of the greatest Conservative thinkers, wrote that 'a state without the means of some change is without the means of its conservation'. The same remains true, provided we are careful to safeguard 'the balance of the constitution', that always delicate, and all too often vulnerable balance of power between the Commons, the Lords, and the Executive, represented in the late-twentieth century by the Prime Minister.

And perhaps it is this evidence of the growth of executive power lodged in Number 10 that is at the heart of public concern about constitutional reform. Not so long ago, a former Lord Chancellor warned of the danger of the emergence of 'an elective dictatorship'. Recent developments have done nothing to allay the fear. On the contrary, successive developments have only re-inforced concerns that the 'balance of the constitution' is being destabilized as power is concentrated in an ever-diminishing number of hands. If true, it provides a powerful argument not for retaining the Lords in its present form, but for reforming, and thus re-empowering the Upper House, the more so in view of Labour's huge majority in 'the other place', and the widely per-ceived quiescence of the Labour backbenchers in the Commons.

The dangers implicit in such a situation are clear, and it is interesting to speculate on whether Labour's proposals for the reform of the Lords are part of a wider plan to neutralize criticism of the executive; of whether the centralizing tendencies already widely commented upon are a reflection of Mr Blair's taste for a Presidential style of government, without the safeguards that are built into the US constitution. A paranoid notion? Possibly, but then Labour's current, two-stage proposal for reform is the most disturbing feature of the entire project, that in proposing to strip hereditary peers of their powers to vote, they have failed to answer the crucial question: What form will the reformed House take? Are Labour honest in their intentions, or as some critics suggest (and they are by no means all Tories) could it be that their reticence on the subject disguises a more deep-rooted ambition to emasculate the Upper House and turn it into little more than an ennobled quango?

Lloyd George, no friend of the Upper House, once described the Lords as the poodle of the Conservative leader, Mr Balfour: 'It fetches and carries for him. It barks for him. It bites anybody that he sets it on to'. History is full of ironies, and it would be darkly ironic if the Lords was to become Mr Blair's poodle, to bark and bite at his beck and call. Not, as I say, that I am opposed to reform. Clearly, the Upper House needs to come to terms with the challenges of the twenty-first century, rather than making an icon of its past, the trouble being that, at times, the past takes on material form.

* * *

The State Opening of Parliament is a great occasion which, as a newcomer to the House, I was determined to attend. I rose early, donned my robes, and was in the Chamber a couple of hours before the ceremony began. At first, the place was almost empty, but slowly the benches began filling up, and as their Lordships entered I played the game of best-guessing who would take the seat next to me, this one or that one or the old gentleman who was shuffling his way down the floor of the House and studying the place with a kind of rheumy intensity before climbing the gangway and taking the still vacant seat. The smell was of mothballs, as if his Lordship had been disinterred from some long-distant past, and between wiping away the tears from my eyes I said: 'Good morning, my Lord. I suppose you've been to lots of State Openings before?'

His reply was as dusty as his appearance: 'Indeed not. The last time I attended was thirty years ago.'

'Then may I ask why you've come today?'

'Well, it's this fellow Blair. He's going to do away with us hereditaries, so I thought it'd be good to get a sight of the chap before I'm abolished.'

The laugh that followed had wrinkles on it. Apparently the notion amused him, and momentarily I shared his amusement. If he found the idea of his own abolition entertaining, then why shouldn't I share in the joke? Or could it be that I laughed to disguise the embarrassment I felt that he represented precisely why there were proposals afoot to 'do away with us hereditaries?' And as I listened to the Queen's speech, I wondered how all this had come about. How was it that Labour now commanded such a huge majority? What had caused the electoral disaster of May 1997? Was it that the Conservative Party had come to believe in its own infallibility, in the conceit that after eighteen years in power they were the natural Party of government, or was there more to it than that?

The simple answers were manifold: that the Party had run out of steam; that it was 'time for a change'; that it was irreparably damaged by the tide of sleaze that appeared to have engulfed it. No question, each contributed powerfully to the debacle of May 1997. But they were by no means all. The explanation lay deeper than that. I know John Major well, and am a great admirer of his. He is a very honest, upright, straightforward sort of man, and if he has any one weakness it may be that he is too decent for his own good. Everyone has their Achilles' heel, and in the last couple of years of his administration I don't think that he was tough enough on the Euro issue, and the troublemakers on his own backbenches. In my time at Tesco, I had a great bunch around me, nonetheless I had to knock a few heads together occasionally, and I think that if John Major had been a bit more ruthless, a little less forbearing, and chopped out some of his friends early on, the election results might well have been different.

Not that we would have won. Public opinion was running too strongly against us for that, aided and abetted by a generally hostile press, and the spin that Labour placed on their policies. Indeed, the measure of Labour's sleight-of-hand was that they succeeded in selling Conservative economic policies as their own, and that Tony Blair stood on what was, to all intents and purposes, a Conservative platform which led people to say: 'OK, we'll give this guy a chance. He's not Old Labour and he isn't going to do anything too radical like raising our taxes, so what the hell, let's give Labour a whirl.'

In short, we were beaten at our own game, in part because of the internal wranglings that racked the Party, in part because we had lost touch with our grass roots. One thing I learned during my time in retailing was that it was people that our business was about; that once you start getting a bit uppity and thinking that you know best, that's when your troubles begin. And the same applies to politics. Customers or constituents it makes no difference. Ultimately both are in the people business which is something that the Conservative establishment tended to forget. Indeed, there was a certain irony in the fact that for all their differences, they nonetheless continued to believe in the Party's political ascendancy, to its cost.

I don't think that it is an exaggeration to say that Black Thursday, 1997, traumatized the Conservative Party, and I know that John Major was deeply hurt by the disaster. After eighteen years it seemed inconceivable that the electorate had rejected Conservatism so decisively, by such a huge majority, and it took the Party a year and more to come to terms with the fact that it has to listen to what people are saying if it is to re-build the electorate's confidence in its policies – not least on the crucial question of whether or not Britain should become a full partner in the revamped European Community.

Frankly, I find it very hard to go along with William Hague's views on Europe. It is all very well to play the game of 'wait and see', but for half a decade and more? No businessman I've ever known would put himself out of play for all that time. Of course, even the Labour Party can't decide on whether to go in or not and like so much else, continues to fudge and mudge on the issue. While there is something to be said for suspending judgement to see how the first tranche goes, however, it is not a question that can be ducked indefinitely. Yet that's exactly what Hague seems to be doing, and to me that's absurd. True, a hundred and one things can happen over the next ten years, but it is nonsense to think that if we pretend hard enough the future will simply go away. It won't. At sometime or another, the Party will have to make up its mind on the European issue, or remain the victim of the internecine feuding that has proved so damaging in recent years. And meanwhile? Meanwhile, if we have to move, then we should be preparing to make the move now. My own business contacts certainly share the same view.

But whatever the outcome, one thing is already inescapable: Europe now exerts extraordinary influence on the entire culture (economic, social, political) of the UK. However hard we may wish it, that reality will not go away. Like it or not, we are inextricably involved in the European project, and the more influence we can bring to bear on containing the influence of the Brussels bureaucracy, the better for all concerned. In fact, if I have one, overriding reservation about Europe, it is the unacceptable nature of the power vested in the hands of the Eurocrats who, all too often, are accountable only to themselves. Twenty years have passed since Mrs Thatcher talked of driving back the frontiers of the state, the danger being that supra-national power may now be replacing national power, without the checks and balances essential to safeguard Burke's 'balanced constitution'.

And if this is my substantive reservation, it is reinforced by my experience of the operations of the Common Agricultural Policy during my time at Tesco. When Britain first considered joining Europe, Barbara Castle campaigned vigorously against entry on the grounds that it would raise food prices. She was right. Depending on which of the EU's statistics one cares to choose, the CAP continues to absorb either 46.8 per cent or 54 per cent of the European budget, yet rather than reducing prices to the consumer, this multi-billion pound subsidy has inflated them by destroying the competition by which prices are kept low.

Which is not to say that I am anti-farmer. How could I be? As a staple of my business career, I recognize better than most the uncertain and often hazardous nature of farming. Indeed, as Chairman of Tesco, I was very keen on farming co-operatives working closely with multiples to establish a better flow-line between the farm gate and the supermarket shelf. Once farmers came to understand that we were not out to fleece them, and that they were going to get a fair and guaranteed return on their produce – in short, a reverse of Jack Cohen's principle of screwing his suppliers down to the floor – they were quick to recognize what could be achieved by cutting out the middleman in the supply chain and dealing directly with us. Arguably, in fact, the initiative did something to hold down prices inflated by the CAP; of the market compensating for the distortions caused by the regulatory system.

In practice, of course, there's clearly a place for both, as with the proposed establishment of a Food Standards Agency in the UK. Since Tesco spearheaded the campaign for nutrition labelling in the 1980s, much has happened, especially the public's growing awareness about food standards and safety. A government initiative designed to focus attention on these issues, the new Agency – a combination of public and private sector elements – will play a key role in reforming the organization and development of food policy in the UK.

And there's that word again, reform: reform of Europe; reform of the Common Agricultural Policy; reform of the Lords. No question, we are living in interesting times, and no question, either, of the need for change if we are to face up to the challenges of the twenty-first century. For make no mistake about it, we are entering an uncertain future, and unless we try to think through the problems that it poses constructively, it will compound the uncertainties that lie ahead.

And that's precisely what worries me about the present

clamour for the root-and-branch reform of the Lords, that to date there is little indication that the issue has been thought through carefully enough. Committed, as Labour is, to change, the Party is in danger of adopting a knee-jerk response to an ideological shibboleth, not least as far as some of its younger Members are concerned. I have always liked Mark Twain's story of the four-teen-year-old who regarded his father as a fool, and his surprise on discovering when he reached twenty-one just how much his father had learned!

A cautionary tale, it is something that many of the new intake of MPs would do well to remember: that experience is not some-thing that can be lightly discounted, and it is just this, experience, that the Lords has to offer. What has struck me most forcibly about what has been called 'the finest Club in Europe' is the unique concentration of experience to be found in the Upper House, in the arts and education, in the law and in business, in science and medicine, in government itself. You name it, and the expertise is there in the Lords, the problem being to redefine its role and, thus, ensure that it continues to play a constructive role in tomorrow's world.

On this, at least, there is general agreement, the question again being: What form should the reformed House take? After a life-time spent in questioning received opinions, I'm in no position to romanticize about what was at the expense of what-should-be. Jack Cohen taught me the dangers of looking over my shoulder at some figmentary past. At the same time, however, I learned that there is no point in discarding what you've got until there is something better to put in its place. Yet this is just what Labour seems to be hellbent on doing. In proposing to abolish hereditary peerages without revealing the precise details of what's to come next, they are playing blindman's-buff with the future of the Lords. They protest that they are concerned with 'open government' (buzzwords in the Labour lexicon), yet they remain neurotically secretive about their intentions. They maintain that they are concerned 'to modernize our constitution', yet the suspicion remains that their covert sympathy for a nominated Chamber would lead to an unacceptable increase in Prime Ministerial patronage.

Even the present Lord Chancellor, Lord Irvine, appears to be aware of the danger, having warned of the need to avoid the perception of creating 'the biggest quango in our nation's history'. He is not alone. The concern is widespread. Indeed, at times, it seems that Labour is entering the future backwards, for the essence of the problem is that before deciding on the future composition of the Lords, the debate should focus on the future role of the Upper House, on its powers and responsibilities rather than on its composition. As on so much else, however, it is an issue on which Labour is notably silent. Historically, the Lords has been a revising Chamber, a watchdog concerned to amend and improve on legislation arriving from the Commons. How is it possible to improve its efficiency in order to play this role? Surely, this is the nub of any reform proposal: that it is only when the Upper House's objectives have been redefined, that its future composition can be determined.

Given that the Lords know what they are about, there is no shortage of choices on offer as to how it could be reformed. Should hereditary peerages be abolished entirely, or should there be a re-entry process for certain hereditary peers? Should either the whole or the majority of the Upper House be elected, or should there be a two-tier Chamber consisting of voting and non-voting peers? Should 'Peoples' Peers' be selected by lot on an annual basis, or should the Lords be composed of a balance between nominated peers and peers elected on a regional basis? Should the Upper House be drastically reduced in size? The

options are apparently limitless, a kind of constitional lucky dip –
you pays your money and you takes your choice.

But if we are spoiled for choice, two overriding factors should
determine any changes that are made, notably, of containing the
Prime Minister's legislative powers by retaining a substantial,
independent element in the Lords. The alternative would mock
the object of reforming the Upper House in order to improve its
performance as a revising Chamber. And this, after all, is what the
entire project is supposed to be about. Whilst the means may differ, it seems to me that there is widespread agreement on the end
to be achieved, though I can't speak for my companion at the State
Opening who anticipated his own abolition.

Possibly, of course, he regarded the whole thing as a joke. And
why not? If their Lordships can't laugh at themselves, then who
can? Or perhaps he, too, thought it was time for a change. Who
knows? I certainly didn't. I've never thought of myself as a revolutionary, but sitting there cocooned in the redolence of mothballs,
there was one thing that I did know: that after eight hundred years
of helping to shape Britain's history, reports of the imminent
demise of the Upper House were premature.

CHAPTER NINE

This Sporting Life: A Quiet Revolution at Lord's

> As Chairman of Tesco for twelve years, I had it easy compared
> with the ordeal to which the likes of Atherton and Stewart were,
> and are, subjected. Twice a year I would go in to bat for the
> company with the publication of the half-yearly and annual
> figures . . . Since then I have learned, second-hand, a little of the
> difference between my own experience, and what it takes to
> cope with the everyday and gruelling pressures of leading an
> England Test side.

PERHAPS I AM a bit of a revolutionary after all, albeit of the quiet
sort. My mother would have been horrified at the notion, but then
how could I be anything else? Since the day when Jack Cohen first
offered me a job, the world has been turned upside down – in
· business, in sport, in everyday life – and simply to survive one has
to be something of a revolutionary. At which I can hear certain of
my fellow peers chuntering over their order papers and wondering what sort of a maverick they've let loose in their midst: 'A
revolutionary Conservative? Absurd! Contradiction in terms!'

They are wrong, however. As I see it, the essence of
Conservatism is not to blow the bugle to advance as a cover for its
own retreat into the past, but to lead from the front. Disraeli once
wrote: 'I have always been of the opinion that revolutions are not
to be evaded'. I can't say better than that. To survive, in fact,

means anticipating, rather than simply reacting to change which is why I question the wisdom of William Hague's policy towards Europe. Maybe there are imponderables in play. Maybe the Euro project will pose problems. Maybe many things. Only one thing is certain: good leadership means forestalling rather than gainsaying the future.

Which sounds very much like one of those management manuals – 'Leadership is a functional specialization, determined by both qualitative and quantative factors which, in turn, are conditioned by their capacity to adapt to exponential change . . .' – that I have foresworn. Nonetheless, the principle still holds good: that the future won't be denied. And never more so than in sport. Almost sixty years have passed since my father bought me my first cricket bat, not one of those tip-and-run affairs, but a genuine five star, with Patsy Hendren's legend emblazoned on the blade. Ridiculous as it sounds, I suppose that bat was my first love affair, and I'd sand it, and oil it (but never on the splice), and stand it in the corner of my bedroom, waiting for tomorrow. And when tomorrow came, my father and I would pace out the wicket in our Hinchley Wood garden, and I'd take guard, and a Freeman-cum-Larwood-cum-Verity he'd trot up to the wicket to bowl me leg breaks, off spinners, googlies, Chinamen of every variety until my mother called me in: 'Time for bed'.

Those summer days seemed endless, a childhood idyll, and if I listen carefully I can still catch the echo of my father's coaxings, promptings, admonitions: 'Forward, that's it, forward . . . Good, Ian, good. Now let's try something a bit different . . . Remember, eye on the ball.' As if I could forget. A gentle man, and infinitely patient, it was he who first taught me to love the game, and not just cricket. At prep school I was already more interested in soccer, cricket and rugby than in work. That was for swots, and subsequently I've often wondered whether my parents really got their money's worth out of their investment in my education. They were not well off, and sacrificed a great deal to give me a private education, where I excelled in everything but my studies, but then the public school culture was very different from what it is today.

Nowadays, academic achievement is the yardstick of excellence, whereas in my time to 'play for the First' was invested with a sort of mystic significance. Godlike figures, we would strut the quad, each with our train of falsetto-voiced admirers: 'What a header! What a try! What a score!' Or possibly not, as the case may be. Possibly we were simply fooling ourselves, for I sometimes wondered just how all those A. N. Others felt on being regimented to line the boundaries of our exploits, of whether they begrudged us our all-too-brief moments of glory. Probably not. The culture was too deeply engrained for that, not least as far as I was concerned.

I suspect that I would never have made much of an academic, though I did learn a lot from sport. If any two characters helped shape my future, in fact, it was two masters at Malvern: George Chesterton and Dennis Saunders. The one, a cricket Blue who had played for Worcestershire, the other, a soccer Blue and a former England amateur international, were both, in their time, deputed to teach me geography. A desperate occupation, I didn't envy them the task.

Out on the sports field, however, it was very different. I captained both the cricket and soccer sides at prep school, and had already won a place in both teams within a couple of years of arriving at Malvern. In retrospect, I suppose it was wrong that a fourteen-year-old should find himself playing alongside seventeen- and eighteen-year-olds, but there I was – Macker MacLaurin – playing at inside-left in the soccer XI, and coming in at number seven or eight in the batting order. Not that I had any complaints about being so lowly placed in the line-up. Goodness knows, I was proud enough to be there at all, until that day George Chesterton came up to me in the pavilion:

'Ian, what do you think is a good score?'

What could I say? Modesty forbade that I should inflate my prospects, but then there was always my vanity to think about: 'Well, sir, I suppose that twenty-five or thirty wouldn't be a bad knock.'

To this day, I've remembered his reply: 'You're in this side as a batsman, and when you go to the wicket you've got to think about scoring a century, not twenty-five or thirty. It's never any use settling for second best. Always play to the best of your abilities, so don't talk to me about twenty-five or thirty, when you should have a century in your sights.'

A century in my sights! At fourteen years of age, the notion sounded preposterous, but George's remonstrance has become the text for my life – never to settle for second best, but always to keep a century in my sights. In a funny sort of way, of course, it may do something to account for the fact that I've always been my own most serious rival, that I have always been in competition with myself. I'm no amateur psychologist, after all, I've had more to do than to start analysing myself, but I do suspect that the will-to-win is inbred, one of those dominant genes that conditions our personalities before we've even begun, the enigma being: How is it possible for a competitive individual like myself to put together and work with a team?

Frankly, I don't know, though I think I caught a glimpse of the answer during the last Ryder Cup match at Valderrama. There is no more competitive or individualistic game than golf, and the closer you get to the top, the tougher and more individualistic it becomes. I've been lucky to play in Pro-Am tournaments with such greats as Lee Trevino, Tom Watson, Gary Player and Nick Faldo, and even then the killer instinct was there. And that was just for fun. When it comes to the majors – the Masters or the Open – the sheer intensity of competition is palpable, an electrifying thing.

Which was how it was at Valderrama. Man for man, I think that if you had matched the Americans against the Europeans you would have had to say that the Americans had the stronger side. What they fielded in talent, however, they lacked in team spirit or the will to win. Twelve great players, they just couldn't put it together as a team. Which was where the Europeans had the edge. All great individualists, they wanted to win that much more passionately than the Americans, and none more so than Seve Ballesteros. Perhaps it was his Spanish pride, or perhaps it was memories of the rough treatment that had been meted out to him as a young player on the US circuit that motivated him, all that's certain is that for the duration of the tournament he succeeded in fusing his players with the collective will to win. For me, that was leading from the front. I know that Seve had his critics, and possibly he was over-demanding, possibly he did drive the team too hard, but whatever the case, Europe won.

After what seemed to be an eternity of slugging it out in appalling weather conditions, it was a moment of explosive release. Everyone was caught up in the excitement, the players laughing and crying and embracing one another, as their exuberant caddies threw themselves into the lake that flanked the seventeenth. And as I stood there watching, it seemed for an instant as if time had gone into reverse, and there was Dennis Saunders, always a formidable figure, and all the more formidable when angry. Malvern had been playing Oxford University Authentics, a very strong side indeed, with Bill Brown, the amateur international, in goal. Time was running out, and there was still no score, when I ran on to the ball, with our striker virtually unmarked on my right. I passed. He shot. We'd scored, and in a burst of excitement, we ran to embrace one another, to be separated by Dennis in furious mood: 'If I ever see you doing that again, I'll cut your hand off. You're here to score goals, not to make exhibitions of yourselves'.

How times have changed. Not that there is any point in being judgemental, for it's impossible to turn back the clock to those, now seemingly far-off days, when I captained the cricket and soccer XIs at Malvern. Like the culture they represented, they have gone for good, and whilst the culture had many failings, I certainly learned a great deal from the experience of putting together eleven, skilled players and welding them into a team. Indeed, it has conditioned all that I've done since. The analogy that comes to mind is that leading a team is like playing at outside half in a rugby XV which, in essence, is what I have been all about: acting as a fulcrum for the rest of the various teams with which I have played, and distributing the ball so that they can take the tiger by the tail. And as the worlds of business and sport become ever more specialized, the role of the outside half becomes ever more important, the link man or woman who provides direction for all the rest.

It is all very well management gurus wrapping up their theories in gobbledegook, but as far as I'm concerned, that's the real criterion of good leadership. Not that I'd thought the matter through when I left Malvern. Far from it. Philosophizing about anything, least of all about sport, was not my forte. I may have walked tall at school, but two years of National Service was a levelling experience, and while I had a great time playing cricket for the RAF and soccer for the Corinthian Casuals, there was always the unanswered question: What comes next? Civvy Street jobs weren't hard to come by in the 1950s but at twenty years of age, I had as little taste for business as I had an appetite for sport. For as long as I could remember, cricket and soccer, and to a lesser extent, rugby, had dominated my life and with the conceit of my years, I decided to give them a go.

While my father was Scottish, and my mother was Welsh, I was born in Blackheath, and they were both keen that I should play for Kent. Those were the days when residency counted for something, and although I was never able to make out whether I was a man of Kent or a Kentish man, I was nonetheless invited to play for the County, to play first for Kent Young Amateurs, then for Kent Second XI, both punctuated by games for the MCC. Those were great times, as were the times I played soccer for Chelsea's Combination XI. As I soon learned, however, there is a vast difference between playing school, club, and county cricket. So much may seem obvious, but it's only when you've been out there, in the middle, that you come to appreciate how great the difference really is. You are playing to the same rules, yet you are playing a different game. It is no longer simply a matter of skill, rather of mental toughness. Whilst you may be able to play all the shots, and maintain a good line and length, that's only the half of it. Ultimately, cricket is a form of psychological warfare, and the higher the level, the more punishing the battle for the mind becomes.

Sometimes the apparent languor of the game disguises its sheer intensity, for Americans raised on the crash-bang-wallop of baseball to wonder whether cricket is really a game at all, not some quaint Old English pastime devised to while away the hours between opening times. They couldn't be more mistaken. Indeed, nothing differentiates our two cultures more than our approach to cricket, a game of which Neville Cardus once wrote: 'Cricket can mean much to a man: responsibility can weigh down the strongest'. And if anything is to test a player's fibre, it is to play for England. Whoever first applied the word Test to that first match between England and Australia in 1880 was right. They are, indeed, the acid test of a player's character, demanding a quantum leap not so much in his skills as of his mindset.

Once I thought that perhaps I could make it, that perhaps I had what it took to reach the top. We all have our dreams, and that was mine: of MacLaurin I. C. (the last of the gifted amateurs) scoring a maiden century for England, and the crowd rising to their feet as I raced up the Oval steps waving my trusty sixer with Patsy Hendren's legend engraved on the blade, while Jim Swanton intoned in voice-over: 'Magisterial performance . . . Recalls the young Hutton, Hammond, Compton . . .', and then, as I entered the pavilion, the voice faded, and the dream died. Fantasies are all very well as far as they go, but they are no match for reality, and the reality was that I was fooling myself, and it was then that after a short spell as a salesman with Vactric, I met Jack Cohen in the bar of the Grand Hotel, Eastbourne.

And that was that, the end of my fantasies. For the next thirty years I had no time to indulge them, so I stowed my gear and hung up my boots, and took to golf, arguably the most infuriating yet enthralling game ever devised. It is not so much that one is playing against one's opponents, rather against oneself, and although I eventually achieved a nine handicap, I always believed that next time, or the time after that, there would be one golden round when I would better my best – and there were the old fantasies again!

Tesco had always fielded a team in the various competitions organized by the trade, and when I became Chairman I decided that the company should run its own Pro-Am tournament. Manufacturers were the dominant players in the sponsorship field, but I felt that it was only right and proper that as one of the most successful companies in the UK we should plough some money back into the economy through a sponsorship budget. During my time with the company we raised millions for various charities, not least through our Pro-Am tournament. Played on the Monday following the last day of the Open, it has attracted some of the leading players in the game, and has raised upwards of £1.8 million for various charities. In fact, I can still remember the look of delight on Princess Anne's face when I handed over a cheque for £250,000 for the Save the Children Fund, back in 1994. Perhaps my fantasies were not so misspent after all, or my indulgence in golf!

* * *

In the late 1970s, Ann and I bought a house in Spain within a chip shot of two excellent courses: the Las Brissas and Aloha clubs. One morning we were out on the ninth fairway at Las Brissas together when there was a shout of 'Fore', and a ball shot over the trees from the first tee, to be followed by its owner. There was a momentary stand-off and then 'Mac?' he said, and 'Brian?' I replied, which was how Brian Davis and I came to renew a friendship that had been in abeyance since we'd left Malvern more than thirty years before. Neither of us had changed all that much, though he was able to hit a golf ball straight when we were at school! Over drinks we talked-up old times until it was time to go, when he invited me down to play at Valderrama.

And that's how I came to meet Jimmy Patino. The stories about the man are legend, not least, of his love affair with the Valderrama. Together with friends, he had been a long-time member of the old course at Soto Grande, and most mornings they would meet for coffee before going out to start at the fourth. Eventually, the course became so popular that they couldn't get on at the fourth, and had to join the queue to start at the first. This was too much for Jimmy and his friends, so they decided to buy and improve the other local course, the Las Aves. All went well for the first year, then Jimmy presented his partners with a bill for the improvements that had taken place. Their reaction was identical: 'Hold on Jimmy, you are spending all this money on the club, but as far as we are concerned enough's enough, and if you want to continue, that's strictly up to you.' Which is how he came to buy out his partners, and set about achieving his ambition of transforming what is now the Valderrama into one of the finest courses in the world. And he has come close to doing that too, for there are few who would question the fact that it is now the finest course in continental Europe.

Indeed, it was largely because of Jimmy's vision that Valderrama came to host the Ryder Cup. Both he and I were involved with the Professional Golfers' Association European tour, and had partnered one another as European observers in the first round of the Ryder Cup at Kiawah Island in 1991. After the game, we retired to the Johnny Walker tent for a Scotch, where Jimmy raised the question of the Valderrama hosting the next Ryder Cup match in Spain. I was all for the idea: 'Compared with this course, Valderrama is fantastic, and if you like I'll make the pitch for you.' It was a spur-of-the-moment offer that I've never regretted. How could I? Europe's victory over the Americans in 1997 redeemed all the time and effort that the small team that I assembled spent on devising, and then refining, the presentation on which we made the pitch. When the decision was announced and Jimmy heard the news he was ecstatic. It was the end of the beginning of an odyssey that culminated on the eighteenth green at Valderrama six years later.

In that one moment, all the backroom effort that had gone into pitching and preparing for the match paid off, and as a bystander I could only reflect on the contrast between the professionalism that had made first the match, and then the victory, possible and the bureaucratic nightmare I found on being appointed Chairman of the UK Sports Council in 1995. The invitation to take up the post came from Ian Sproat, then Minister for Sport, and what reservations I had about taking on the job, were quickly justified by what I found on accepting the offer.

In theory, the Council was established to run sport in the UK. In practice, it had been impotent from the outset, neutered as a result of virtually all financial power being vested in the English, Scottish, Welsh and Ulster Sports Councils. While it was all very well for them to run their own budgets, it meant that the UK Council was virtually powerless and, in consequence, had degenerated into little more than a talking shop, to my own and Howard Wells' intensifying irritation.

A dynamic character, Howard could hardly credit what he discovered on taking over as Chief Executive of the Council, having spent fifteen years doing the same sort of job in Hong Kong. As far as he was concerned, the contrast between the two operations defied belief – the one a kind of indoor Four Nations championship refereed by a Council without a pea in its whistle; the other a model of how sport should be administered – and I can still hear him raging with frustration:

> The Council's a farce . . . When I took off for Hong Kong they were talking about reform, but nothing's changed . . . It's the same old, bureaucratic shambles that it always was . . . But then, what d'you expect? . . . How the devil did they hope to create an effective operation when the Council was set up by the same people who had run the old one? . . . The last thing they wanted was change . . . Their sole concern was to perpetuate their own hegemony . . . The thing's a disgrace, living proof that there's life after death.

And who was I to disagree? The situation was as sad as it was hopeless: sad because of what it meant for the well-being of sport;

hopeless because there seemed to be little will to change an operation that was seriously flawed. On a couple of occasions, I told Ian Sproat that what was needed was to turn the entire business on its head and provide the Council with some real muscle in order to develop an integrated programme for sport. It made little difference, however. The system was too entrenched for that, and so the talk continued, interminably and ineffectually, each side talking up their own case, and all uniting only in their determination to frustrate the Council's attempts to impose some kind of order on the farrago that passed for the administration of UK sport.

For someone who had been used to making things happen, it was an unhappy time for me, and one of the few reasons why I welcomed the return of a Labour government in May 1997 was the knowledge that as a Conservative peer there was little likelihood that the new administration would reappoint me as Chairman of the Council. It took only three days to confirm my suspicion. Asked of what prospects I had of retaining the job, Tony Banks, the new Minister of Sport, was reported variously as saying that my support for the Conservatives hadn't done my career with the Council any good; and that our association would be 'interesting but very short'. There was no mistaking his intention, and rather than be fired, I got my retaliation in first and resigned.

In retrospect, it may have been that we were both a bit precipitate. Indeed, when we did meet, Tony Banks apologized for his off-the-cuff remarks – 'the trouble with me, Ian, is that my brain doesn't always engage with my mouth' – and said that given the chance, we probably could have worked well together. And maybe we could, for he is the sort of chap who has got the balls to say 'Enough is enough,' as far as the bureaucratic shambles that is the UK Sports Council is concerned and, in the process, enhance rather than prejudice the future prospects for sport in this country.

Not that I don't appreciate the problems he faces. I do. After more than two years as Chairman of the England and Wales Cricket Board, I know the difficulties involved in changing people's attitudes, even when the future of the game they love is at stake. In fact, it was for precisely this reason that I became the agent for change. Forty years ago, I would have given my right arm to play for England, and to me it is still The Game. But nostalgia for 'the times when . . .' is no substitute for reality that in the increasingly competitive environment of world sport, cricket has to come to terms not so much with the twentieth as with the twenty-first century. When I turn my back on reality, of course, I, too, regret the passing of those 'times when . . .' knowing that they will never return. How can they? It is no longer possible to capture the somnolence of John Arlott's poem *Cricket at Worcester, 1938*, when: 'Drowsing in deck-chair's gentle curve, through half closed eyes, I watched the cricket'.

Those times are long gone, yet it's not easy to exorcize nostalgia, or the mindset that it encapsulates. Indeed, I caught a glimpse of the conservative ways of the England cricket establishment long before being appointed Chairman of the ECB. Besides being a member of the Middlesex Committee, I had been a member of a number of MCC committees, including the General Committee, since the 1980s. In those days, the Club was a pretty crusty sort of organization, and as a newcomer to the General Committee, I was hesitant about raising my voice too loud in case I should be overheard! Finally, however, an issue arose about which, at the time, I felt very strongly. I can't remember exactly what it was; all that I do know is that I felt compelled to speak. All the great and the good were there in the Committee Room, and as the meeting progressed with all the urgency of a wake, I racked up my courage until the moment arrived when I caught the President's eye. Opening for England had nothing on the occasion, and whilst what I said was probably immemorable, it certainly succeeded in provoking Field Marshal the Lord Bramall's ire: 'MacLaurin, this is a cricket club, not bloody shops'.

Jack Cohen, you should have been living at that hour, the justification for your strictures of so many years before: 'and if that didn't bloody well work, I'd pull the whole lot down and build a supermarket'. Not that his Lordship's attitude was unique. On the contrary, it reflected the predominant attitude of the cricketing establishment at the time. And as I was soon to learn, it takes time to change such attitudes. It was in the summer of 1996 that I received the first of a series of calls asking whether I would allow my name to go forward as Chairman of what was then the Test and County Cricket Board. I was enormously flattered that they should even consider me for the job; at last I'd have the chance of 'playing for England', the only trouble being that I was already involved in a punishing workload.

The callers, however, were persistent. Seemingly, they wouldn't take 'no' for an answer, and at the fourth or fifth call I said: 'OK, I'll tell you what I'll do. If I'm the only name you can find I'll do it, but I'll be doing it reluctantly because I've got a lot else on my plate'. And that, I thought, was that, but that's where I was wrong. Some five or six weeks later, Brian Downing, the TCCB's Chairman of Marketing, rang me: 'Guess what, Ian, there's no one else standing, so we'd like you to do the job'. And what could I say but that I'd give it my best shot? Which is how I came to chair the last meeting of the TCCB in December 1996. Traditionally, the Board's meetings had been leisurely affairs, lasting for a couple of days, with seventy or eighty people present. It was an impossible way to do business, and my first act as Chairman was to impose some discipline on what, for so long, had been a talking shop, with the result that we wrapped up the meeting in three hours, and on 1 January 1997, the England and

Wales Cricket Board took over from where the TCCB had left off.

If the event marked the end of the *ancien régime*, however, the mindset remained, as I discovered all too soon. The England side were touring Zimbabwe, and when I rang the Board's offices at Lords to say that I would like to join the tour, the first question I was asked was where I would like to stay. There was only one thing I could say: 'With the team, of course'. A shocked silence greeted my reply, which was matched only by my own disbelief on being told: 'But that's never happened before. The management always stay in a different hotel'. It did not take me long to find out why. On arriving in Harare, Ann and I were driven to the team's hotel, and were horrified by what we found. Our own room was bad enough, but the team's quarters were even worse: two players apiece to each pokey room in which, at best, the air-conditioning worked to a regime of its own. And this in a climate where the daytime temperature often reached 110 degrees. Small wonder that the management preferred the luxury of either the Michels or Sheraton Hotel to the accommodation provided for our players.

And small wonder, either, that it was proving to be such an unhappy tour. If I'd believed that the old distinction between gentlemen and players was a thing of the past, the Zimbabwe experience quickly disabused me. Possibly, I was naive, but I honestly thought that the team would not only be well cared for, but also that the management would provide it with some sense of purpose, direction. In both cases I was wrong, for when I asked Mike Atherton who had discussed England's game plan with him when he was first appointed captain, he looked me straight in the eye and said: 'Chairman, you are the first person who has ever talked to me about it'. And the evasive reply I received when I put much the same question to the coach, David Lloyd, was even more revealing: 'Chairman, I don't think I should be talking to you like this', at which he refused to say anything further.

Why not? What was there to hide, or was it simply that Mike Atherton was right, that there was, indeed, no game plan? So much for my naiveté, and looking back now, I'm convinced that much of the blame for our poor performance in the Test series was due, in part, to the failure of management to provide the team with decent leadership, in part, to the miserable treatment meted out to our players when they were off the field. Touring is a tough enough occupation at the best of times – three or four months away from home, separated from wives and girlfriends – without players having to cope with the apparent indifference of a management to the everyday conditions in which they are expected to live. In such circumstances, it is hardly surprising that, just occasionally, players go off the rails, as they did a couple of times in Harare, to the unfeigned delight of the media.

There was a circus of journalists following the tour, not all of them genuine cricket correspondents. Some were just out to get a story, any story, as long as it made the headlines. And what they could not expose, they fabricated which, as I've learned to my cost, isn't unusual. Indeed, I get really choked off reading pieces that bear no relationship whatsoever to the facts, snide pieces like the one that appeared recently which said it was time that I polished up my act. The basis for the charge was that as the guest of honour, I had failed to turn up for a dinner in the Commons, and hadn't even troubled to apologize for my absence. The truth was very different. I had written to the organizers well beforehand apologizing for being unable to attend, explaining that I would be in hospital at the time.

At times, it seems that such fabrications are limited only by the imagination of their authors, especially when it comes to the coverage of cricket. Patently, cricket needs to obtain coverage, informed coverage, the danger being that, in the process, it comes to be regarded as fair game for the paparazzi, with all the razzamatazz, with all the hype that that entails. Of course there are still a lot of great journalists around, journalists who know the game and love it – Christopher Martin Jenkins, Richie Benaud, Bob Willis, Alan Lee, David Gower, Jonathan Agnew, Ian Botham, Mark Nicholas, to name but a few – but in their wake there is always the rat-pack, as the England team learned to its cost in Harare. I'm not saying that the media were responsible for all that occurred, but they certainly made the most of our time of troubles, which was terribly sad, for as the Chairman of the Zimbabwe Cricket Union told me on the evening before my departure: 'We were looking forward to England's visit so much, but now I've got to say that we're glad to see you go'.

It was a damning indictment not so much of the players, more of the way in which the whole tour had been conducted. As far as I was concerned, such a foul-up could never be allowed to happen again, and the newly appointed Chief Executive of the ECB, Tim Lamb, agreed entirely. An Oxford Blue, who played first for Middlesex and then for Northamptonshire, Tim had few illusions about the state of the game, or the magnitude of the task we had undertaken. And the deeper we probed, the more disturbed we became. As we soon discovered, in fact, the Zimbabwe experience was symptomatic of much else, of the two worlds each inhabited, separately, by players and management, and I can still recall a conversation I had with the Warwickshire player, Nick Knight, about how he had first received the news of his selection for England:

'How did you first hear that you'd been selected?'

'I was driving from Warwickshire to Somerset to play in a Sunday League game when my mobile rang. It was the Sports Editor of the *Daily Mirror*, who asked me how I felt about being picked for the England squad.'

'Nobody had been in touch with you before that? No one from Lord's rang you with the news?'

'No, that was the first I knew about it, and I could hardly believe what I'd heard.'

'And then?'

'Well I turned up at Old Trafford the following Wednesday, and Ray Illingworth, [then the Chairman of the Selectors] was parking his car at much the same time. I thought he might say something, but I don't think that he even recognized me.'

'So when did you pick up your England cap? Who presented it to you?'

'No one. There was this box on the table in the dressing-room and I just took one that fitted me.'

As a commentary on the way in which the game was run, Nick's recital appalled me: that what should have been one of the great moments of his life had been reduced to wondering whether or not the Chairman of the Selectors even recognized him; of having to grub about in a box on the dressing-room table to find an England cap that fitted him. Only a few, a privileged few, get to play for England, yet it was as if, having once picked a team, the selectors had no further responsibility for their actions, that win or lose it was no business of theirs. A lesson in leadership by default, it was hardly surprising that England had not won a five-match Test series for more than a decade.

A case of, 'Forward men, we are behind you', the English cricket establishment laid claim to everything except its own shortcomings. Of course, there were always excuses to account for our failures, but all too often it was Them (the players) rather than Us (the administrators) who were held to be at fault. While it is nonsensical to pretend that good management can transform England's performance, it is equally nonsensical for critics such as Matthew Engel to rubbish any attempt at reforming what, patently, was a flawed operation, to say in effect: 'To hell with the management, let's get on with the game'. We got on with it for too long, and the results spoke for themselves.

Obviously it is not possible to quantify what might be called 'the management factor' when it comes to determining the outcome of a Test series. All that is certain is that it does have a part to play in ensuring that, in future, England teams have the off-the-field support they deserve; that they are not subjected to the kind of shabby treatment to which they were exposed in Zimbabwe, are not subjected to the sort of humiliating experience that Nick Knight described to me.

How was it possible to create any sense of team spirit when the Them and Us attitude was so pervasive? What hope was there for a team's morale when the England team was treated in such a cavalier fashion? The answer was, there wasn't. God knows, it demands enough of any side to play out a five-day Test, without having to play against the management as well.

And what goes for a team in general applies in particular for the captaincy. There is no more exposed position in sport. You name it – soccer, rugby, hockey – the captain's out there on the field for ninety minutes at most, not for six hours a day, for five days on end, six hours of five days during which their every move, their every decision is scrutinized, analysed, criticized not only by the aficionados, but also by the wiseacres who tune-in, world wide, to the blow-by-blow account of their ordeals. And at stumps, the media is always there, hungry to make headlines of whatever they may happen to say: 'Adam Holioake's last stand? Glory, glory Alec Stewart. Mike Atherton's long good-bye.'

If spectating and commentating are forms of sadism, then one has to be either a hero or a masochist to take on the job of captaining England. However well our Test sides perform, it seems that they could always do better, while when they lose it is all too often the captain who is condemned to the kind of equivocal obituaries in which the media revels: 'Too good for own good to have been offered captaincy . . . Wasted brilliance . . . Outstanding in everything, but capacity to lead . . .' I've always thought that in damning with faint praise, the media damns itself.

As Chairman of Tesco for twelve years, I had it easy compared with the ordeal to which the likes of Atherton and Stewart were, and are, subjected. Twice a year I would go in to bat for the company with the publication of the half-yearly and annual figures. Just occasionally the going could get rough, just occasionally I was bowled a bouncer, though not often, and however tough the going, I always knew that come twelve o'clock I would go off for lunch, and not have to return for another six months. And even that seemed all too soon! Since then I have learned, second-hand, a little of the difference between my own experience, and what it takes to cope with the everyday and gruelling pressures of leading an England Test side.

In fact, I was not altogether surprised when Mike Atherton decided that he wanted to stand down as captain following England's defeat by Australia at Trent Bridge in 1997. He had been having a pretty torrid time with the bat, and getting a huge amount of stick from the press not just for his own, but also for England's performance in the series. In such circumstances, who could blame him for wanting to quit, though the first I knew of his intention was when David Graveney, the Chairman of Selectors, called me on my car phone to say that he had resigned. The news really shook me. I couldn't believe that Mike's resignation was in his own or in England's best interests, and all I could say was that I'd give him a call at his flat in Manchester to try and persuade him to reconsider his decision. When I did so, however, he was adamant:

'Yes, I've resigned. I've had enough and think that the captaincy would be better held by someone else.'

'Well, d'you want some advice from me?'

'Sure, I'll always listen to you, Chairman, but I'm a stubborn Lancastrian and won't change my mind.'

'All right, but at least hear me out. We appointed you for the whole summer, not two-thirds of it, and if my business experience is anything to go by, and you quit now, it'll be seen as a triumph for the press, and not your decision. All I can say is take the side to the Oval, and after that we'll sit down together and decide what to do. If you decide then that you really want to go, you can do it in your own time and with dignity, rather than being bludgeoned into it by the media.' But it did no good.

'No, I've made up my mind, and that's the end of it.'

All I had left was to play for time. 'Look, I'm in my car and will be home in an hour or so, at least think over what I've said till then.'

Which he did, and when I rang he said: 'I don't want to fall out with you, Chairman, so OK, I'll stay.'

I don't remember exactly what I said in reply – something about, 'Whatever you do, you won't fall out with me. I admire you too much for that.' All that I do know is that he took the side to the Oval where, to be polite, England played on a doubtful wicket to win the game in three days, only for the media to perform yet another about face.

In reflecting on those couple of phone calls, I think that Mike's crisis reflected in microcosm the crisis in English cricket in 1997. It was a punishing year – first Zimbabwe and New Zealand, and then the Australians – yet it taught me a lot about how not to do things, even if it took time for the new order to replace the old. So much, of course, was inevitable. It was simply not possible to change the mindset of the establishment over night. The old practices, the old prejudices died hard. For all that, however, there could be no going back to times when an England side was expected to tolerate the conditions to which they were exposed in Zimbabwe.

If Tim Lamb and I were resolved on any one thing, it was that such wretched treatment was going to stop; that if we were going to rebuild Team England, then all the old practices, all the old prejudices should be consigned to where they belonged – the past. And not before time. There is a certain irony in the fact that cricket is regarded as the quintessential English game, and yet for so long so many of our finest players continued to be patronized by gentlemen who didn't seem to give a damn for their welfare. Or perhaps it was just that, that it was so quintessentially English, that it reflected, precisely, the difference between Them and Us.

Whatever the case, it was as damaging to the morale of English players as it was to England's prospects of fielding a winning XI, which was why the situation could not be allowed to continue. If England was to continue competing at the top level, things had to change, and that is why our Test teams now receive the sort of support and respect that is theirs by right. Rather than having to endure the intolerable conditions to which they were subjected in Zimbabwe, touring sides now get the sort of accommodation they deserve. Rather than hearing the news by chance, every player now receives a call from David Graveney, either congratulating him on being selected for the England squad, or explaining why he has been dropped. Rather than having to grub around in a box in the dressing-room, they are now formally presented with their England caps by the captain on the field of play before a match begins. Small things, perhaps, but cumulative, and all part of an attempt – a long overdue attempt – to give players the recognition they deserve for what they have achieved. When, that is, they have earned such recognition, and that applies as much to their approach to the game as it does to their cricketing skills, for the two are synonymous.

Compared with the Australians and South Africans, too many of our players lack the toughness, the mental resilience, the sheer bloody-mindedness that it takes to win. Instead, they are inclined to go soft when the going gets rough. Why? God knows, we have more than enough professionals, upwards of 400 at the latest count. Yet, at best, only thirty or forty have the makings of Test players, which is absurd. Once again, why? What's gone wrong?

Ultimately, the counties have a huge responsibility for running their own staff, and bringing a bit of discipline into the game. All too often, however, that has not been the case. Some time ago I visited a county ground where the Chairman was deploring the turnout of his players: 'What are you going to do about them? Look at them, they're a bloody shambles'. And he was right, but what could I say, other than: 'Hold on a minute, Chairman, you're the guy who is in charge here, not me'. If my reply surprised him, I, in my turn, was not altogether surprised by his attitude. In fact, it tended to confirm my suspicion that rather than being the centres of excellence which they should be, a number of counties – but too many for the well-being of the game – were little better than breeding grounds for a kind of devil-may-care complacency. Which, in itself, was not surprising. How was it possible to generate any real sense of competitiveness in a situation where the tail-enders in the County Championship were playing-out the season in games watched by two men and a dog?

The answer was, it wasn't, and in such conditions it was hardly to be wondered at that players didn't take either themselves or the game sufficiently seriously, or that youngsters, such as Andrew Flintoff, were occasionally inclined to get a bit above themselves. No question, Flintoff's a fine young player, the trouble being that his approach to the game doesn't always match up to his talents.

In the autumn of 1998, the England A squad spent a couple of days team-building together at a retreat in the Lake District. A medical check was one of the prerequisites before they left on tour, which everyone passed, except Flintoff. Warned by Simon Pack, the International Teams Director of the ECB, that he had better do something about it, he was given a couple of weeks to get himself into shape. When he turned up for the second check, however, he was in even worse condition than before. Not that he seemed to care, for on hearing the news he scoffed at its implications: 'OK, what are you going to do about it, give me a couple of hundred lines?' Thankfully, he has learned his lesson since then, and made an outstanding contribution to the England side that toured Zimbabwe and South Africa in early 1999 and, as such, thoroughly deserved his selection for the England World Cup squad. An English superstar in the making? I certainly hope so.

In fact, if management is having to rethink its role, then players will have to rethink their approach to the game, not that I don't appreciate the problems facing many of the youngsters who achieve what amounts to instant stardom. It takes a great deal of maturity to cope with success, and many young players are simply not equipped to live with the pressures of being lionized by the media, idolized by the fans, and surrounded by a court of adoring bimbettes. Oscar Wilde wrote that he could resist anything, except temptation, and heaven alone knows, there are temptations enough for players to get above themselves in the pressurized world of sport. It seems like half a lifetime ago that I saw George Best play, and only yesterday that I was reading of how Gazza had been found weeping on Stevenage station. Each brought his own, particular magic to the game, to be consumed by his own success.

Indeed, there is a terrible irony in the fact that so many great players who have 'made it' too young have been broken by their own talents. And here again, the counties have a huge responsibility for protecting their younger players from over-exposure, and in consequence becoming too big for themselves. But if young players have to develop the maturity to handle their success, it is equally important that they develop the mental fibre, the toughness which is a prerequisite for winning at the top level. And what applies to our up-and-coming players applies equally well to everyone who wins an England cap. Until they toughen up their act, England will remain where it has been for far too long, at fifth or sixth in the world rankings – and no one loves a loser.

Quite the reverse, which is why, that Sunday afternoon of the 1998 Test at Trent Bridge, when Mike Atherton took on Allan Donald at his most demonic was, for me, the most memorable session of the South African series. Win or lose, Mike showed the sort of guts that are needed if England is to win the test of the future. Not that Mike's was an isolated performance. In fact, England's display during the series not only made the doom-watchers swallow their predictions, and helped to encourage hesitant sponsors that their investment in the game was well spent, but also showed the crowd appeal of a winning team, more than 10,000 spectators turning up on the last day at Headingley to cheer Team England on to their first, five-Test series win in twelve years.

Trying to create, or rather to recreate, Team England was only one element in the job of trying to put to rights the problems of England's cricket, however, which was why, in the summer of 1997, the Board published *Raising the Standard*. As a mission statement, its terms were straightforward – to provide a base which would secure England's place as the most respected and successful cricketing nation in the world – and in practical terms it advanced a step-by-step development plan for the game, from schools and clubs and up via the Counties to the Test arena. In fact, if there is one thing above all else which I find encouraging, it is that, for all the Jeremiahs, there are now 1.5 million youngsters playing the game, and that some 400,000 are girls. It is with them that the future lies, and the key to that future lies in providing them with the sort of encouragement and support that is needed to capitalize on their enthusiasm.

In September 1997, 95 per cent of the proposals included in *Raising the Standard* had been accepted, but in the media storm that followed the Counties' rejection of 5 per cent of the programme, all the rest was forgotten. Jealous of their independence, the First Class Forum appeared careless of the fact that the first-class game was close to bankruptcy; that in 1997 not one of the eighteen Counties was solvent, the best of them, Lancashire, being only some 85 per cent self-sufficient, the worst of them covering less than 30 per cent of their running costs. Without their average annual £1.2 million income from the ECB, in fact, the majority of the Counties would have been bowled out long ago.

However hard one juggled with the figures, those were the facts of life, yet it seemed at times as if those responsible for managing the first-class game were paralysed by the reality. Which was nothing new. There had long been talk of the need for reform, but for all too long it remained just that: talk. On the learning curve involved in taking on the Chairmanship of the ECB, I worked my way back through *Wisden* and came across a 1968 report of Leslie Deakins, then the Secretary for Warwickshire, in which he based his case for reform on the fact that in the previous twenty years County cricket had lost 80 per cent of its audience. That was thirty years ago, thirty years during which talk of reform had all too often become a substitute for action. True, there had been piecemeal changes, but they had never been adequate to cope with the escalating crisis facing the game.

Indeed, as I read back through my copies of *Wisden* it struck me that everything had changed, yet everything remained much the same; that the game, or rather, its management, was stuck in some sort of time trap. It was all very well for the members of County Committees to indulge their fantasies that given time the good times would return. The fact was, they wouldn't, though they were loath to admit as much. Yet when it came to reforming the first-class game, it was with the County Committees that the real power lay. Under its terms of reference, the ECB Management Committee is responsible for the overall administration of cricket in this country, with the notable exception of the First Class Forum made up of the eighteen First Class Counties and the MCC who have the right to veto any decisions taken by the Board that affect the Counties' autonomy in the crucial areas of finance and the domestic playing programme.

Effectively, this means that unlike any normal business, where a company's strategy is determined at the centre and its subsidiaries are expected to comply, the ECB Management Committee is subordinate to the First Class Forum when it comes to the crunch of decision-taking. This is not the place to argue the case for reversing what I regard as an administrative anomaly, simply to note the difficulties involved when it comes to trying to create a coherent strategy for the future of the first-class game; when it comes to trying to achieve any unanimity of purpose amongst eighteen County Committees each proud of their own history, and all operating to their own agendas.

During my first couple of years as Chairman of the Board, in fact, it seemed to be a case of eighteen sides playing against the middle which, at times, brought Tim Lamb and me close to despair. No question, there was plenty of sympathy for what we had to say about the need for change, until it came to the fine detail of what such changes involved. No question, the Counties agreed that there was no possibility of reinventing the past, until it came to trying to persuade them to forego their differences in the best interests of the future. Then it was different, very different. Then all the old differences as to the way ahead emerged, to culminate in the impasse of September 1997, when the First Class Forum rejected the Board's plan for revivifying the first-class game.

Before publishing *Raising the Standard*, it was clear from all the research that we had done that the favoured option was for a two division County Championship, except, that is, as far as the First Class County Chairmen were concerned. They wanted nothing of the idea, and it was clear to Tim and I that at least fourteen of them would vote against it. Nonetheless, something had to be done, and urgently, which is how we came up with the idea of the Conference system, under which the Championship would be divided into three equal Conferences with end-of-the-season play-offs. It was the first time in my business career that I had gone against all the available research, and it was a decision which I later came to regret.

Whatever my reservations, however, the Conference system was tabled and published in *Raising the Standard*, to be thrown out at a meeting of the First Class Forum. Seemingly, the impasse was complete, and in an attempt to break the deadlock the two-division proposal was raised again, and I came out and endorsed the idea. The meeting eventually ended as it had begun, without any substantive decisions having been taken, except to hold a further meeting in a few weeks' time. Unfortunately, I went on a holiday to Spain during the break to find that when I came back yet another scheme had been devised: to have an all-play-all County Championship with the top eight playing in a Super Cup in 1999.

I'll never forget that Black Monday meeting of 15 September 1997. How could I? Only a couple of days before, Yorkshire had played Kent in a match that could determine the outcome of the

County Championship, yet fewer than 1,500 people had turned up at Headingley to watch the game. If anything argued the case for change it was evidence such as this. In the event, however, it made little difference. The meeting began at 10.00 a.m. and by lunchtime I knew that we had lost. After six months researching and formulating our proposals, the Board's recommendations for a two-division Championship were thrown out by a 12 to 7 vote by the First Class Forum who opted, instead, to favour what came to be known as the Radical Status Quo: the all-play-all Championship, with the Super Cup additive.

As Ian Botham was to say: 'It's a terrible day for English cricket ... I think we are in the biggest mess we've been in. We've had the chance to put it right, but these people live in their little ivory towers. The biggest problem is that they think the game is for members. It's not. It's for the whole country.' I couldn't have put it better: ivory towers indeed. A survey conducted by the Professional Cricketers' Association had revealed that a significant majority of their members were in favour of a two-division championship, a finding reinforced by the Board's own soundings among the general public, yet the majority of the County Committees, representing at most 150,000 County members, wanted nothing to do with the scheme.

As far as I was concerned, the all-play-all formula was a solution that resolved nothing, and that Monday evening I remember thinking: 'What the hell, if they're bent on writing an obituary for first-class cricket, then why should I bother?' The trouble was, I did. While there were rumours in the press that I might resign the Chairmanship, however, I'm not the resigning sort (save, that is, from the UK Sports Council!) or the sort to leave a job unfinished. In the previous year, Tim and I had made huge strides in re-organizing the administration of the game, and we were damned if we were going to quit the process now, even if it meant returning to the drawing board and going through the whole process of resubmitting our proposals. Next time around, however, we wouldn't repeat the mistake that had scotched our original plan which included everything except the costs involved in doing little or nothing at all. Next time around, there would be no ducking the financial facts of life, though in itself this provided grounds for controversy.

If the Board raised the income critical to underwriting the losses incurred by the Counties, then the Counties, in their turn, could say that it was they who were providing the players for Team England on which the Board relied to generate the cashflow from sponsorship and TV to cover their own financial shortfalls. Paradoxically, part of the answer to the problem lay in the problem itself: that unless we could improve the performance of Team England, and make the first-class game more attractive, there was a very real risk that sponsors would pull the plug on their investment in the game.

In fact, that was already happening. Until England's victory over South Africa, and under intensifying competition from other sports, there was already evidence that cricket was losing its commercial appeal. In short order, AXA had withdrawn their sponsorship of the Sunday League, Texaco had pulled out of the one day internationals, and Britannic had decided that they could no longer afford to sponsor the County championship. They were all very nice about it, of course, but there was no escaping the fact that as one of their marketing gurus remarked: 'The trouble is that as far as most people are concerned, cricket's become a spectator sport for oldsters, and they're a dying breed'. Unless something was done, and speedily, it could well have become the requiem for the first-class game.

If the loss of a substantial sponsorship income helped to concentrate the minds of the Counties on the complex question of financing the game, however, it also helped to reinforce the Board's determination to strike the best deal possible when it came to re-negotiating the contract for TV coverage of the game when the existing contract came up for renewal in 1998. But here, again, we faced a problem. Having been placed on the government's A list, which effectively restricted live coverage of Test cricket to terrestrial channels, it limited the Board's freedom to deal, and in all probability meant that only the BBC would pitch for the contract. Consequently, the Board was hamstrung, unless we could change the government's mind, and persuade it to transfer Test cricket from the A to the B list, which would open the field to all-comers.

As we were quick to learn, this involved much more than a shift in administrative detail. The BBC had been in the business of covering cricket for more than half a century, and emotions ran deep at any suggestion of transferring the game to the B list. The arguments advanced against making such a move were manifold, but one underlay all the rest: that the entry of new and, quite possibly, more predatory bidders might restrict the TV coverage of the game to only those fortunate enough to have access to satellite channels. Certainly, the issue was one of Chris Smith's major concerns. As Secretary of State responsible for sport, he made his position quite plain when he met Terry Blake (the ECB Marketing Director) and I: 'Look, if there is going to be any change, I'll have to be certain that there will be a decent amount of Test cricket on terrestrial TV'. We sympathized with him entirely, as I suspect he sympathized with the case we made for the Board: 'As you know, cricket is not a rich sport, and we do need more money for the running of the game, but as things stand it's damnably difficult to hammer out a decent deal when it involves negotiating with only one interested party'.

Chris Smith's decision to transfer cricket from the A to the B list was a courageous one. It would have been all too easy for him

to say: 'You're on the A list, and that's where you'll stay,' instead
of which he was subjected to the kind of media flak of which I had
my share: 'MacLaurin sells out to Sky; Mac the Knife zaps Beeb.'
As is so often the case, the headlines anticipated the outcome of a
deal that had yet to be struck. Three contenders entered the lists
for the new, four-year contract – the BBC and Channel Four, both
of whom wanted all the Test matches, and Sky who wanted two
Test matches and all the one day internationals. All three made
outstanding presentations, but as we were leaving our meeting at
the Television Centre, Brian Downing told the BBC team that
while the Corporation had done a superb job for the game in the
previous sixty years, they simply weren't in the ballpark as far as
the money was concerned.

And he was right. The bid by Channel Four, which in total
topped the BBC bid by several million pounds, amounted to an
offer the Board couldn't refuse, more especially because they
ensured that six out of seven future Tests would be shown on terrestrial channels by Channel Four. Not that the deal was just about
money. The new agreement not only provided the Board with
opportunities to screen Test highlights in the early evening, but
also to market the game on other channels. As Chris Smith was to
say when he heard the news: 'I'm delighted with the decision. I'd
have got terrible stick if you guys had let me down'. And I was
delighted, too, that we hadn't broken faith with him, though I still
couldn't get my head around what had been going on at the BBC.

The word was that the Corporation was spending over £30
million a year on its rolling news service which was being watched
by little more than 1 per cent of the viewing audience and yet it
couldn't put together a bid that would have given it at least a
reasonable chance of winning the Board's contract. Or possibly it
was just that, that having spent so much on its News 24 channel,
the Corporation simply didn't have sufficient cash to secure the

on-going coverage of a game that commanded a loyal and massive following.

Of course, the case was not unique. Far from it. Once *Grandstand* was a must for anyone keen on sport, providing first-class coverage of soccer, rugby and Grand Prix racing. Where are the old crowd-pullers now? Gone. Today, *Grandstand* is little more than a shadow of what it once was, the poor relation of TV sports coverage. Which is sad as much for what it reveals about the management priorities of the BBC as for what it says about the management of the Corporation itself. Indeed, when the results of the new contract were announced, a House of Commons Committee lambasted the Corporation for its 'lazy and arrogant' approach to sport, comments which I wholeheartedly endorsed.

While the Board had struck a good deal as far as both the financial returns and the coverage of cricket were concerned, the decisive question remained to be answered: Had the Counties re-thought their approach to the reforms proposed by the Board? The First Class Forum meeting was scheduled for October 1998, and this time there could be no fudging and mudging the issue. This time the financial facts of life would be there for all to see, and the choice would be theirs. Either the First Class Forum could accept the Board's recommendations, or retreat into its own imaginings, a Never-Never land in which Old Father Time plods his way into a future on which the sun never sets.

Thirteen months had passed since the First Class Forum had rejected the ECB's proposals for reviving the fortunes of First Class County cricket, thirteen months during which the Board had gone a long way towards implementing 95 per cent of the proposals advanced in *Raising the Standard*. Now all that remained to be seen was whether the Counties would buy into the remaining 5 per cent of the Board's plan. Logically, they had no alternative, but even logic has its limits, and when I attended the First Class

Forum's meeting in October 1998, I wondered, for a moment, whether we had got it right, whether there wasn't something to be said for retaining the status quo. After all, perhaps the Counties did know best. Perhaps they were right after all.

A tough and independently-minded bunch of characters, there could be no disputing the fact that the eighteen County Chairmen and the MCC representative knew and loved their cricket, or that they had done a formidable and often thankless job for the game down the years. Surely, such collective experience couldn't be written-off lightly? Surely, there was some alternative to the revolution that the Board was proposing to implement? Then the meeting was called to order and what reservations I had disappeared. However attractive it might seem, there could be no going back to the past, for there could be no mistaking the significance of the presentation by Terry Blake, a vivid scenario of vanishing spectators, falling County memberships, and a rising age profile of those who still continued to watch the game. It was, frankly, a *tour de force*, and as Terry went on it became increasingly clear that if things continued as they were the first-class game would be in very serious trouble indeed.

And the Chairmen could not help but agree. Whatever doubts they may have harboured, they could no longer escape the reality of the incipient problems facing County cricket. Terry's message was as clear as that, change or else . . . and after two days of talking, two days which I rate among the toughest yet most constructive of my time on the Board, the meeting agreed to a package of measures that will transform the first-class game: measures to increase the number of home Tests and one day internationals; to contract a spread of England players to the ECB, a decision, incidentally, that has yet to be finally ratified; to introduce a new, 45-over National League in the 1999 season, and to reduce the Nat West Trophy from 60 to 50 overs.

After two years of coaxing and cajoling, headbanging and arm twisting the Board had finally succeeded in raising the standard. But one issue remained to be resolved: the $64,000 question as to the future of the County Championship. Would the County Chairmen reverse their previous decision and go for a two-division championship, or would the old orthodoxies prevail? All the signs were propitious at the October meeting, but a final decision was postponed until December, and meanwhile all I could do was to wait and to wonder. Those two months seemed interminable as I juggled the options and tried to read the future. The Counties had come so far, but would they go that little bit further?

I need not have worried. Having nerved themselves to change, the County Chairmen were in no mood to compromise with the past when they finally met to discuss the future of the County game in December 1998. With two Counties abstaining, they voted 15 to 1 in favour of establishing a two-division County Championship, an historic decision heralding the most radical change in the structure of the first-class game since the Championship was first rationalized in 1890. This was, indeed, a quiet revolution. First-class cricket would never be the same again. As I left the meeting, however, I knew that this was only the end of the beginning, rather than the beginning of the end.

True, the Board has achieved its original objectives, but that didn't mean that now it could rest on its laurels. The job of securing the future of English cricket will never be complete. True, the Counties have recognized the imperative for change, but that didn't mean that like the dormouse in *Alice in Wonderland* who slept between courses, that they could now go back to sleep again. The whole essence of *Raising the Standard* was to provoke administrators throughout the game to 'think long' in order to improve the performance of English cricket, from grassroots level upwards, and thus the performance of Team England. Ultimately, in fact, all depends on that, on re-establishing England's Test credentials not only to attract new sponsors to the game, and to ensure that next time around, the Board will be able to strike a good deal when it comes to renegotiating its TV contracts, but also to reviving the public's flagging interest in the game, and here, for a final time, the Counties bear a huge responsibility for ensuring the future welfare of English cricket.

In 1998 the First Class Forum turned its back on the past, but there is a great deal more that needs to be done. It is no longer any use the Counties regarding themselves as rest homes for the aged, and if that sounds tough, the fact is that they are not in the charity business. It is no longer any use the Counties indulging young talent and, in consequence, ruining it, and if that sounds harsh, the fact is that young players have to earn what they get. It is no longer any use the County Committees running the game like gentlemen amateurs, and if that sounds tough, the fact is that professionalism is now the name of the game. Maybe the notion is unpalatable, but the truth is that amateurism has long passed its sell-by date. Maybe we regret the passage of time, but we can no longer afford to live in some mythical past if, and here the paradox, English cricket is to recover its pride and become the force that it was in 'the good times when . . .'

But then, once one begins to play the 'If' word we are back to fantasizing again – if only rain never stopped play, if only Down Under was Upside Down. In fact, all that I know for certain is that while he was never known to have played cricket, Disraeli was right – revolutions are not to be evaded – and although my mother may well have been horrified at the idea of her son turning quiet revolutionary, I suspect that my father would have had other ideas: 'Good, Ian, good, now let's try something a bit different.'

CHAPTER TEN

Reflections

> . . . if there is one thing I have learned from the past, it's that there is no future in standing still. And never more so than today. Things are changing too quickly for that: in business, in sport, even in the Lords.

OCCASIONALLY I WONDER whether the Vactric salesman that I once was could ever have imagined where he would end up when Jack Cohen first offered him a job. Probably not. Most probably all that he thought about was the prospect of earning a thousand a year and having a car, a fantasy far removed from the reality of 'piling it high and selling it cheap' at Tesco. Occasionally, however, our memories catch up with us, as they did not so long ago. There was I, Lord MacLaurin (and the title still takes me by surprise), Chairman of the England and Wales Cricket Board (and I can still remember that long ago day at Lord's when Jack bearded the great and good of the game) laying down the law about the future at a Lord's Taveners luncheon, when I caught myself wondering: 'Hang on a minute, who the devil am I? How did I come to be here?'

Appropriately enough, it was my driver, Jim, who had the answer. The lunch over, he had gone out for a quiet smoke when one of the other guests tackled him about my speech: 'I don't know why we have to put up with blokes like MacLaurin. Who is he anyway, some character who thinks he knows it all simply because he was born with a silver spoon in his mouth.' Jim and I have been on the road together for twenty-five years, and I suppose that he knows me better than most people. Down the years, in fact, he has been my alter ego as much as my driver, and as I heard it later, his retort was in keeping with his character: 'Sorry, but you've got it all wrong. The Governor didn't begin with a silver spoon in his mouth, but with a broom in his hand sweeping out Tesco stores.'

I suppose that as we get older we all get lumbered with an image, yet we still have to live with our past. And that's the hardest part, making the connection between what was and what is. It is now forty years since my wife, Ann, first climbed into the deckchair in the back of my clapped out, Vactric van, and I still wonder if she knew what she was letting herself in for, or realized what it implied when I told her, all cock-a-hoop, that I had landed a job with Tesco. God knows, her father had made it clear enough to both of us that the company was a no-go area, but I was too cocksure to care. After all, if life is not about taking risks at twenty-two years of age, then it never will be.

Which is easy enough to say when you have been as lucky as I have. Indeed, I sometimes suspect my own good fortune and wonder whether I'm really who I am and not some bloke who happens to have arrived at his present destination by accident, a bit like G. K. Chesterton who found himself at a country railway station and telegraphed home: 'Am at Princes Risborough. Where should I be?' In a way it is a question that encapsulates all the rest, that we no sooner arrive than it is time to move on, the question being: To where? Of course, there are no easy answers, but if there is one thing I have learned from the past, it's that there is no future in standing still. And never more so than today. Things are changing too quickly for that: in business, in sport, even in the Lords.

A little while ago I was entering the House when one of the

hereditaries was leaving. A venerable figure who might well have given Methuselah a couple of years, the attendant asked whether he required a cab, or an ambulance. The joke must have been a long-standing one, for both of them laughed. For an instant, however, I caught myself thinking: 'Surely this isn't how I'll end up, counting down the time until someone whistles up a cab, or an ambulance, for me'. There was more to the moment than that, however, for as I stood there in the shadow of the House it seemed as if the incident was a metaphor not so much for the institution, as for my own experiences of its arcane practices.

When John Major invited me to become a working peer I was both honoured and delighted: honoured as much for what the tribute meant to all those thousands of people at Tesco who had taken the tiger by the tail as for what it meant to me; delighted because I really believed what he had said, that I would, indeed, be a working peer. Ann has always called me a workaholic, and she is better qualified to judge than most, and as my time at Tesco ran out, I often wondered: 'Is this where the future comes to a halt?' Then came that invitation, and as the cliché has it, it was an offer I couldn't refuse. Now I would have something useful to do. Now I would have a future. I was soon to be disillusioned. Having taken an office close to the House, and an apartment across the river from Westminster, I settled down and waited for the work to begin – and waited, and waited, but nothing occurred.

I had been asked to do a job, but it seemed that the job didn't exist, or myself for that matter. As far as the Conservative Whips were concerned I could just as well have been a non-person. An absurd situation, it flouted the most basic principles of good management. There was no briefing by the Whips' Office, no attempt to explain what role, if any, I could play in the business of the House, nothing, in fact, but the seemingly interminable wait for something to happen. And even when there was something which

I could do, the silence of the Whips' Office was deafening. First there was my maiden speech which, apparently, no one wanted to include on their agenda. Then came the fiasco of the sports debate, one subject on which I thought I was well qualified to speak, except, that is, for the Conservative Whips. Apparently, they wanted nothing of me, and finally in a spasm of frustration, I tackled the Chief Whip, Lord Strathclyde, and asked him straight: 'What about this work that I was supposed to do?' The question startled him, but not half as much as I was startled by his reply: 'We are still in shock after the last election' (which had taken place more than a year before) 'and maybe you would be more useful to us back in business'.

The advice was superfluous. Frustrated by what I had found in the Lords, I had already been appointed Chairman of Vodafone, and become a non-executive director of Whitbread, besides taking on the job at the ECB. Nonetheless, the question remained: was this really why I had been asked to accept a peerage, to go back into business? The answer defied all that I had been led to believe, that I would, indeed, be a working peer. As far as I was concerned, it wasn't a happy experience. On talking it over with my fellow back-benchers, however, I soon learned that I was by no means unique. Like myself, they had regarded it as a great honour to be invited to sit in the Lords, and like myself, they had quickly discovered that the House lived up to its reputation of being 'the finest Club in Europe', but like myself, many of them wondered why the devil they were there. Recruited as working peers for the expertise they could bring to debate, they were quick to learn that as far as work was concerned, the word was a misnomer. However impressive their titles, the reality was that they had joined the ranks of the titled unemployed! No one, and certainly not the Conservative Party, can afford to waste such talent, which is one lesson among the many that the Party can learn from New Labour.

When I attend debates these days and see Labour's working peers sitting opposite on the government's front bench – life peers recruited for the expertise they, too, can bring to the business of the House – the contrast to the treatment meted out to our own life peers dismays me. It is not so much old habits, but old privileges that die hard. Indeed, if a case can be made for reforming the Lords, then a case can equally well be made for reforming the mindset of the Conservative establishment in the Upper House. Not that the condition is exclusive to the Lords. As my old sparring partner Archie Norman, Chairman of Asda and MP for Tunbridge Wells, has discovered, much the same condition applies in the Commons. An enormously talented businessman, with a great track-record behind him, he sometimes despairs of the innate resistance he meets when there is talk of reorganizing the Party on businesslike lines – as Labour has succeeded in doing.

In fact, it sometimes seems as if the roles of the two Parties have been reversed, and not only in political terms, for not so long ago the joke was that Labour was not one party but two, and even then, that the two bits were at odds with themselves. No longer. Like it or not, one has to give New Labour credit for making a whole of the parts, and in the process, proving that the Party is fit to govern. Of course, the transformation didn't take place overnight. How could it? There were too many shibboleths, too many egos at stake for that, but what Neil Kinnock began, and John Smith progressed, Tony Blair and his team realized – first, with the creation of a highly professional political machine, then with the landslide election victory of May 1997. Once, maybe, the Labour Party was something of a joke. Today, the laugh is at the Tories' expense.

Possibly, of course, the Party is still complacent after its long term in office, or possibly it is still 'in shock' from finding itself in opposition. Whatever the case, one thing is certain: that unless the

Party gets its act together, and quickly, there is a very real risk that it will become the victim of its own shortcomings, a political instance of that-was-the-Party-that-was. At which I can hear my hereditary colleagues protesting that I go too far: 'Damn it, the Party's been with us since God knows when, and before that even . . .' And they toll back the years as if time itself is a talisman, but as I have learned in the forty years since I first joined Tesco, the past is no guarantor for the future.

Jack Cohen thought as much, and came close to destroying what he had created. The English cricketing establishment thought as much, with damaging consequences for the game they professed to love. And now it seems that the Conservative Party is in danger of thinking much the same thing, equally careless of Disraeli's dictum that revolutions are not to be evaded as of the fact that, ultimately, the business of life is more about people than politics. Which, I suppose, is what *Tiger by the Tail* has really been about, ten chapters devoted not so much to discovering my own identity, as to realizing that it is all those people who have populated my life who have made me what I am today, and sometimes I still catch an echo of their voices:

> 'I haven't spent all this money on your education for you to join a company like Tesco . . .'
>
> 'Good, Ian, good. Now let's try something a bit different . . .'
>
> 'Not twenty-five or thirty, but a century . . .'
>
> 'Never forget, the most important bloke in the business, is the bloke on the back door . . .'
>
> 'Knebworth? Knebworth? Tell me a bit more about Knebworth . . .'

Ghosts in the machine, they have all played their part in defining my identity, yet in writing so much about the importance of people, I have neglected the most important people of them all: Ann, and our three children. In many ways, they have been the victims of my success. Certainly, they have benefited from what I have managed to achieve, but there is a price to pay for everything, and it is they who have paid the price for all those times when I was too busy on Any Other Business to devote enough time to them.

For long periods, my workload placed an enormous burden on Ann – of making a home and bringing up the children, with what was, all too often, an absentee husband. Indeed, it was only when she was taken seriously ill some years ago that I realized how much I had taken for granted, that perhaps she wouldn't always be there. The experience brought me up short, and I remember thinking: 'Things have got to change'. As is so often the case, however, good resolutions are made to be broken.

Perhaps that's always how it is. Perhaps it's always a case of promises, promises – until it is too late. Then nothing remains but the realization that broken promises can never be undone, for, only a handful of days after this book was published, Ann died. Careless of my own good resolutions, and forgetful of how close I had once come to losing the one person among all the many people who had contributed most to who and what I am today, I had slipped back into my old, workaholic ways. Indeed, it was only when I left Tesco that we began to make up for those thirty-eight lost years and do all those things that had been foregone for so long. For me, it was a new beginning, and then came the day when there were no more promises left to be broken. And now? Now all that's left is a terrible sadness for what might have been, if only . . .

This is the downside of success, that the people who really count in life are all too often discounted. In the end, I suppose that life is a bit of a balancing act, and I don't think that I've always got the balance right, which is why, in thankfulness for all she sacrificed in allowing me to take the tiger by the tail, I can think of nothing better than to dedicate this book to Ann.

APPENDIX ONE

Profiles

Victor Benjamin: Appointed a Non-Executive Director of Tesco, 1982. Deputy Chairman, 1983–96.

Ron Bronstein: Briefly a Joint MD of Tesco, and Director of the Company's northern operation.

Edgar Collar: Director of Tesco, 1951–62; Vice Chairman of the Company, 1961–62.

Mike Darnell: Joined Tesco 1967; appointed to main Board 1975 as Non-Food Purchasing Director; retired 1994.

John Gardiner: Chairman of the Laird Group, and a former Non-Executive Director of Enterprise Oil, where he met Ian MacLaurin.

Colin Goodfellow: Joined Tesco, 1964; Regional Managing Director, 1973; Head of Fresh Foods Division, 1982; retired 1994.

Jim Grundy: When Tesco took over G&S Food Fare, of which Grundy was the senior partner, Grundy joined the Company's main Board for a brief period.

Donald Harris: Joined Tesco 1964; appointed to main Board 1975 as Director of Computer Division; retired 1984.

Daisy Hyams: Joined Tesco in 1932 as Secretary to Jack Cohen; appointed to main Board 1971 as Director of Purchasing; retired 1982.

Hyman Kreitman: Sir Jack Cohen's son-in-law. A main Board

member of Tesco for quarter of a century, and Chairman of the Company, 1968–73.

Francis Krejsa: Joined Tesco 1960; appointed to main Board 1975 as Director of Property and Estates; retired 1990; Non-Executive Director, 1990–93.

Laurie Leigh: Managing Director of Tesco Home n'Wear, and together with Ian MacLaurin, a Joint MD of Tesco. Laurie Leigh died in 1975.

David Malpas: Joined Tesco, 1966; appointed to main Board as Group Retail Operations Director, 1979; Managing Director, 1983–97.

Jim Pennell: The successor to Daisy Hyams as the Buying Director of Tesco.

Sir Leslie Porter: Sir Jack Cohen's son-in-law, and husband of Shirley Porter. A main Board member of Tesco, 1960–85, and Chairman of the Company, 1974–85.

Arthur Thrush: Director of Tesco, 1961–71.

Dennis Tuffin: Joined Tesco 1966; Regional Managing Director, 1971; appointed to main Board, 1984; retired 1994.

Tesco Statistics
1975–98

Taken from Five Year Records

	1975 £m	1976 (53 wks) £m	1977 £m	1978 £m	1979 £m	1980 (53 wks) £m	1981 £m	1982 £m	1983 (53 wks) £m	1984 £m	1985 £m	1986 (53 wks) £m
Turnover excluding VAT												
UK	501	617	701	953	1,202	1,531	1,821	1,994	2,277	2,595	3,000	3,355
Rest of Europe												
Ireland												
Total Turnover ex VAT	501	617	701	953	1,202	1,531	1,821	1,994	2,277	2,595	3,000	3,355
Operating profit												
UK	23	25	30	29	38	40	51	52	61	69	82	104
Rest of Europe												
Ireland												
Total operating profit	23	25	30	29	38	40	51	52	61	69	82	104
Share of associate												
net interest (payable)/receivable	n/a	n/a	n/a	n/a	n/a	(3)	(16)	(9)	(7)	(2)	0	19
Underlying profit	23	25	30	29	38	37	35	43	54	67	82	123
Market share	n/a	n/a	n/a	n/a	n/a	n/a	n/a	n/a	5.9%	6.2%	6.6%	6.7%
UK full time equivalent employees	26,820	28,782	28,413	30,841	35,302	39,862	38,809	40,421	40,377	40,363	42,020	43,447

	1987 (53 wks) £m	1988 £m	1989 £m	1990 £m	1991 (53 wks) £m	1992 (53 wks) £m	1993 £m	1994 £m	1995 £m	1996 £m	1997 (53 wks) £m	1998 (53 wks) £m
Turnover excluding VAT												
UK	3,593	4,119	4,718	5,402	6,346	7,097	7,581	8,347	9,655	11,560	13,118	14,640
Rest of Europe							0	253	446	534	769	784
Ireland							0	0	0	0	0	1,028
Total Turnover ex VAT	3,593	4,119	4,718	5,402	6,346	7,097	7,581	8,600	10,101	12,094	13,887	16,452

	1987 (53 wks) £m	1988 £m	1989 £m	1990 £m	1991 (53 wks) £m	1992 £m	1993 £m	1994 £m	1995 £m	1996 £m	1997 £m	1998 (53 wks) £m
Operating profit												
UK	145	203	263	317	398	479	552	513	600	713	760	866
Rest of Europe								8	17	11	14	(3)
Ireland												49
Total operating profit	145	203	263	317	398	479	552	521	617	724	774	912
Share of associate												(15)
net interest (payable)/receivable	21	15	2	10	19	65	31	7	(22)	(43)	(24)	(65)
Underlying profit	166	218	265	327	417	544	583	528	595	681	750	832
Market share	7.1%	7.6%	8.0%	8.4%	9.0%	9.4%	10.4%	10.7%	12.0%	13.7%	14.6%	15.2%
UK full time equivalent employees	45,260	50,192	52,742	54,345	59,846	59,519	58,046	60,199	68,552	80,650	89,649	99,997

DTI report:
Guinness PLC

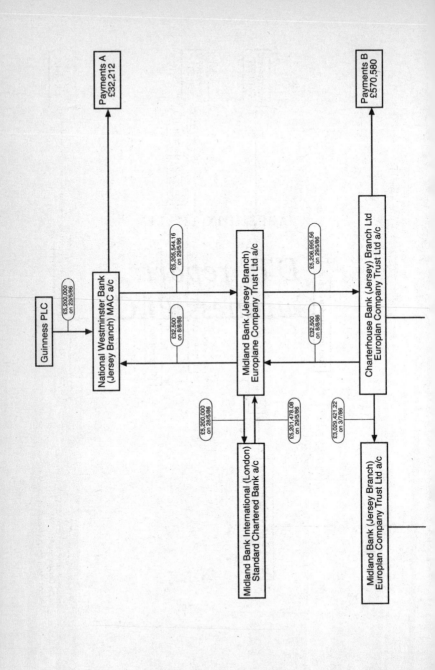

Guinness PLC

£5,200,000 on 23/5/86

National Westminster Bank (Jersey Branch) MAC a/c

Payments A £32,212

£5,205,544.16 on 29/5/86

£32,500 on 8/8/86

Midland Bank (Jersey Branch) Europlane Company Trust Ltd a/c

£5,206,995.56 on 29/5/86

£32,500 on 8/8/86

Charterhouse Bank (Jersey) Branch Ltd Europlan Company Trust Ltd a/c

Payments B £570,580

£5,200,000 on 28/5/86

£5,201,478.08 on 29/5/86

£3,029,421.22 on 3/7/86

Midland Bank International (London) Standard Chartered Bank a/c

Midland Bank (Jersey Branch) Europlan Company Trust Ltd a/c

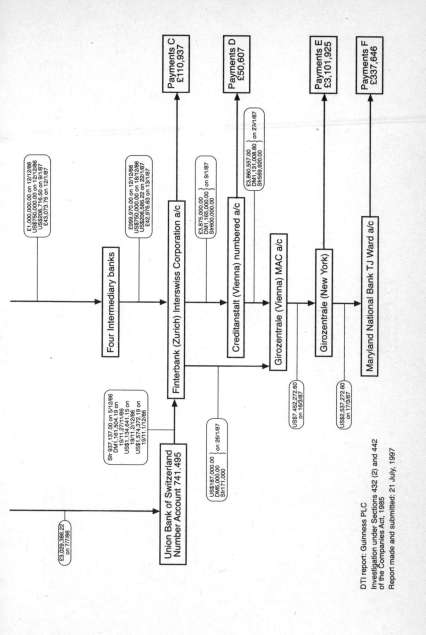

Payments C £110,937

Payments D £50,607

Payments E £3,101,925

Payments F £337,646

£1,000,000.00 on 12/12/86
US$750,000.00 on 12/12/86
US$206,716.50 on 9/1/87
£43,073.75 on 12/1/87

£999,970.00 on 12/12/86
US$750,000.00 on 18/12/86
US$206,585.22 on 22/1/87
£42,976.63 on 13/1/87

£3,875,000.00
DM1,165,000.00 } on 9/1/87
Sfr600,000.00

£3,860,557.00
DM1,131,008.80 } on 27/1/87
Sfr569,920.00

Four Intermediary banks

Finterbank (Zurich) Interswiss Corporation a/c

Creditanstalt (Vienna) numbered a/c

Girozentrale (Vienna) MAC a/c

Girozentrale (New York)

Maryland National Bank TJ Ward a/c

Sfr 937,137.00 on 5/12/86
DM1,161,504.19 on
19/11,27/11/86
US$134,641.15 on
19/11,12/12/86
US$1,574,372.19 on
19/11,1/12/86

Union Bank of Switzerland
Number Account 741.495

US$187,000.00 } on 26/1/87
DM6,000.00
Sfr171,000

US$7,452,272.60
on 16/3/87

US$2,537,272.60
on 17/3/87

£3,029,386.22
on 7/7/86

DTI report: Guinness PLC
Investigation under Sections 432 (2) and 442
of the Companies Act, 1985
Report made and submitted: 21 July, 1997

Index